D0819970

ENVIRONMENTAL DISASTERS

The Mount St. Helens Volcanic Eruptions

Kristine Harper, Ph.D.

☑®
Facts On File, Inc.

The Mount St. Helens Volcanic Eruptions

Facts On File, Inc.
132 West 31st Street
New York NY 10001

Library of Congress Cataloging-in-Publication Data

Harper, Kristine.
  The Mount St. Helens volcanic eruptions / Kristine Harper.
    p. cm. — (Environmental disasters)
  Includes bibliographical references and index.
  ISBN 0-8160-5757-5 (hc: acid-free paper)
   1. Saint Helens, Mount (Wash.)—Eruption, 1980—Juvenile literature.
  2. Volcanoes—Washington (State)—Juvenile literature. I. Title: Mount Saint
  Helens volcanic eruption. II. Title. III. Environmental disasters (Facts On File)
  QE523.S23H37 2005
  551.21'09797'84—dc22   2004059148

Facts On File books are available at special discounts when purchased in bulk quantities for businesses, associations, institutions, or sales promotions. Please call our Special Sales Department in New York at (212) 967-8800 or (800) 322-8755.

You can find Facts On File on the World Wide Web at
http://www.factsonfile.com

A Creative Media Applications, Inc. Production
Writer: Kristine Harper, Ph.D.
Design and Production: Alan Barnett, Inc.
Editor: Matt Levine
Copy Editor: Laurie Lieb
Proofreader: Laurie Lieb
Indexer: Nara Wood
Associated Press Photo Researcher: Yvette Reyes
Consultant: Thomas A. Birkland, Nelson A. Rockefeller College of Public Affairs
    and Policy, University at Albany, State University of New York

Printed in the United States of America

VB PKG   10   9   8   7   6   5   4   3   2   1

This book is printed on acid-free paper.

Contents

Preface

This book is about the eruption of the Mount St. Helens volcano in the state of Washington. On the morning of May 18, 1980, a massive landslide slid down the north side of the mountain. Then a colossal explosion shot out, sending rock, ash, and hot gases into the air. The map on the next page shows Mount St. Helens's location in the southwest of Washington.

Almost everyone is curious about such catastrophic events. An interest in these disasters, as shown by the decision to read this book, is the first step on a fascinating path toward learning how disasters occur, why they are feared, and what can be done to prevent them from hurting people, as well as their homes and businesses.

The word *disaster* comes from the Latin for "bad star." Thousands of years ago, people believed that certain alignments of the stars influenced events on Earth, including natural disasters. Today, natural disasters are sometimes called "acts of God" because no human made them happen. Scientists now know that earthquakes, hurricanes, and volcanic eruptions occur because of natural processes that the scientists can explain much better than they could even a few years ago.

An event is usually called a disaster only if it hurts people. For example, an earthquake occurred along Alaska's Denali fault in 2002. Although this earthquake had a magnitude of 7.9, it killed no one and did little serious damage. But a "smaller" earthquake—with a magnitude below 7.0—in Kobe, Japan, in 1995 did billions of dollars in damage and killed about 5,100 people. This quake was considered a disaster.

A disaster may also damage animals and the environment. The *Exxon Valdez* oil spill in Alaska is considered a disaster because it injured and killed hundreds of birds, otters, deer, and other animals. The spill also killed thousands of fish—which

WASHINGTON

Mount St. Helens

PACIFIC
OCEAN

Columbia River

IDAHO

OREGON

Snake River

The Mount St. Helens Volcanic Eruption

CALIFORNIA

NEVADA

many Alaskan fishers rely on to earn their livelihoods—and polluted the places where the fish spawn.

Disasters are also more likely to happen when people make decisions that leave them *vulnerable* to catastrophe. For example, a beachside community is more vulnerable to a hurricane than a community that is inland from the ocean. When people choose where to live, they are also choosing what sort of natural disasters they may experience in the future; they are choosing the sort of risks they are willing to take. People who live on beaches in Florida know that hurricanes may damage or destroy their houses; people who live in certain areas of California know that earthquakes may strike at any time.

The things that people do to make themselves safer from less dangerous natural events, like heavy rains, sometimes actually make the people more vulnerable to bigger disasters. For example, when a dam is built on a river to protect people downstream from floods, the dam may prevent small floods that would otherwise happen once every 25 years. But when a really big storm occurs—the kind that comes once every 100 years—the dam may not be able to hold back the water. Then a surge of water that is even bigger than it would have been without the dam will come rushing down the river and completely destroy all the buildings in the area.

At first, it may seem easy to blame human disasters, like the *Exxon Valdez* spill, on one or a few people. Some observers blame the spill on the captain, who was responsible for the ship. But perhaps the spill was another crewmember's fault. Maybe the blame should fall on Exxon, because that corporation owned the ship. Or maybe all Americans are to blame, because the United States uses a lot of oil for heating houses and driving cars. Finding the "right people" to blame can be difficult. Is it anyone's fault that people suffer from natural disasters? Natural disasters at first appear to be merely unfortunate "acts of God."

This book and the other books in this series will demonstrate that mistakes people made before a disaster often made the disaster worse than it should have been. But they will also show how many people work to lessen the damage caused by disasters. Firefighters, sailors, and police officers, for example, work very hard right after disasters to rescue people, limit additional damage, and help people get back to their normal lives. Behind the scenes are engineers, architects, legislators, scientists, and other citizens working to design new buildings, make new rules about how and where to build buildings, and enforce those rules so that fewer people will have to risk their lives due to disasters.

The books in this series will show what can be done to reduce the chances that people and communities will suffer from natural and human disasters. Everyone has a role to play in making communities safer. The books in this series can show readers how to become part of a growing movement of citizens and experts that can help everyone make good decisions about disasters.

Please note: All metric conversions in this book are approximate.

Introduction

A volcanic eruption is one of the most frightening events in nature. A volcano can spew tons of hot *ash* and rock into the air and send red-hot molten rock streaming down its sides. The eruption can trigger avalanches of snow and ice, mud and *debris flows,* and *floods* that kill plants and animals in their path.

Although a volcanic eruption is destructive, it is also constructive. The ash that settles over surrounding valleys is often full of nutrients (for example, phosphorus and potassium) that are released as the ash weathers over time. These minerals replenish the soil and enable plants to grow in abundance. If the volcano is on an ocean island, the *lava* flows may actually create new land.

Volcanoes always bring change to the environment. But only sometimes is a volcano a disaster—when residents of the region are killed or injured or lose their homes or places of business. When this happens, a volcanic eruption—like that of Mount St. Helens in 1980—becomes an environmental disaster.

Unlike some other natural disasters, such as hurricanes and tornadoes, volcanic eruptions cannot be predicted. *Volcanologists*— scientists who study volcanoes—are not able to say when a volcano will erupt again. Just because a volcano has not erupted in thousands of years does not mean it is dead. In addition, just because a volcano erupted last year does not mean that it will erupt this year. Scientists can only analyze the data that they collect from instruments that measure movement underground in an effort to understand just what makes a volcano behave the way that it does.

In the meantime, volcanologists work with emergency planners to diminish the impact of a volcanic eruption on populated areas. By using clues that they pick up from examining old lava flows, debris flows and mudslides, and *ash fall* patterns, scientists

Vents atop Mount St. Helens spewed steam and ash that destroyed ice sheets 5 feet (1.5 m) across in explosions that took place in early May 1980. (Photo courtesy of Associated Press)

can predict what will happen during the eruption of any individual volcano. If the volcano is one that produces only slow lava flows, then emergency planners have more time to evacuate people from the danger area. If, however, the volcano is explosive—if it sends out large plumes of ash, hot rock, and gases—then emergency planners have only a very short period of time to get people out of the danger zone. All people living and working in the area need to plan how to avoid the water and mud that may rush down the side of the volcano when the hot rocks hit any ice and snow stacked up on the mountainside.

Although some volcanic eruptions killed thousands of people in the last part of the 20th century, the natural environment is often what is most changed by the eruption. Areas closest to the volcano's *crater* may be wiped clean of all life. Areas just a little farther away may become extremely poor habitats for plants and animals. But no matter how devastated the area looks after the volcano stops erupting, life does come back. Within a few days, insects and plant seeds will fly in on the wind. Eventually, the seeds will sprout, and the insects will build their homes around the new plants. Birds will follow the insects, looking for food. Mammals will also move back to the area—small ones at first, and then larger mammals. Within a few decades, only specially trained scientists will be able to tell that a volcano erupted there.

The Mount St. Helens Volcanic Eruption explains how and why volcanoes form and erupt around the world. The book tells the story of the deadliest volcanic eruption ever to occur in the United States and its immediate and long-term effects on both people and nature. The book concludes with a time line of the eruption, a chronology of volcanic eruptions, a glossary, and a list of sources (books, articles, and web sites) for further information.

Please note: Glossary words are in italics the first time that they appear in the text. Other words defined in the text may also be in italics.

CHAPTER 1

The Nature of Volcanoes

Volcanoes are *vents*, or openings, in Earth's crust that eject lava (molten rock that has reached Earth's surface), gases, and rocks of all sizes. No two volcanoes are the same, and neither are their eruptions. How an individual volcano behaves depends on its type and the kind of *magma* (molten rock beneath Earth's surface) moving within it. Different kinds of volcanoes are highlighted in the "Volcano Types" sidebar on the following page.

As pressure builds inside a volcano, causing new eruptions, lava hardens and forms layers of rock within the mountain, trapping gas in between. This 2002 photograph of the Colima volcano in Colima, Mexico, shows the volcano's crater blocked by hardened lava from an earlier eruption. (Photo courtesy of Associated Press)

Volcanoes occur in three geological situations. In the first case, some volcanoes, like Mount St. Helens, result from the collision of two tectonic plates: an oceanic plate and a continental plate. (*Tectonic plates* are large sections of Earth's crust that are always moving very, very slowly.) As the oceanic plate plunges below the continental plate, the rocks in the oceanic plate melt. The resulting magma then starts pushing its way up through cracks in the continental crust. The "Ring of Fire" volcanoes found on the edges of the Pacific Ocean are all due to colliding plates.

In the second situation, volcanoes occur where two tectonic plates pull apart—this is a geologic feature called a *rift zone*. Rift zones may occur on Earth's surface (for example, in Africa) or on the ocean floor. There are many volcanoes on the ocean floor—they are very deep. After hundreds of thousands of years, the lava from an ocean volcano may build up enough so that the volcano breaks through the ocean surface as an island. Iceland, a country that has several active volcanoes, is the result of volcanic activity on the Atlantic Ridge—the mountain chain that snakes through

Volcano Types

Type and Description	Examples
Shield volcano; broad and dome-shaped; erupts lava flows	Mauna Kea, Hawaii; Mauna Loa, Hawaii
Tephra cone; small with a steep cone; erupts ash and small rocks	Wizard Island, Oregon; Cerro Negro, Nicaragua
Stratovolcano/composite volcano; tall and steep; erupts ash, rock, and lava	Mount St. Helens, Washington; Mount Rainier, Washington

the middle of the Atlantic Ocean, where two tectonic plates are pulling apart.

The third way that volcanoes are formed is by *hot spots*—this is how the Hawaiian Islands were created. Hot spots are locations under the crust that remain hotter than the areas around them. They generally occur under the ocean, because the oceanic crust is much thinner than the continental crust. The magma from the hot spots moves up to the surface through cracks in the crust, slowly building mountains that finally break through the surface of the water. The newest Hawaiian island, Loi'hi, is still 0.5 miles (0.8 km) below the waves. This volcano is being fed by a hot spot approximately 200 miles (320 km) in diameter—the same one that feeds the Mauna Loa and Kilauea volcanoes. According to scientists at the U.S. Geological Survey (USGS), it will take "several tens of thousands of years" before Loi'hi breaks through the surface of the Pacific Ocean.

Until very recently, scientists have generally agreed that hot spots remain in the same place within the mantle while tectonic plates move over them. However, the islands and *seamounts* (eroded volcanic islands that are now beneath the sea surface) that extend north from the Hawaiian Islands do not form a straight line. John Tarduno, a geophysics researcher from the University of Rochester in New York, decided to find out why there was a distinctive bend in the line of old seamounts. By determining their ages and placement on the plate, Tarduno and his colleagues discovered that between 47 million and 81 million years ago, the hot spot was crawling south at 1.6 inches (4.1 cm) per year. According to Tarduno, 47 million years ago, the hot spot slowed down and perhaps stopped, producing the bend. This discovery, published in 2003, implies that hot spots cannot necessarily be used to track movements of tectonic plates. More research will need to be done to see if other hot spots around the world have also moved.

Volcanic Hazards

Not all volcanoes present the same hazards. Shield volcanoes produce very little ash and a lot of lava. Small *tephra* cones just spit out ash and small rocks, while the large stratovolcanoes tend to produce immense clouds of ash, dangerous *pyroclastic flows*, and *mudflows*. Unless a volcano triggers a *tsunami* (a seismic wave in the ocean that can move thousands of miles across the water and send a wall of water onto the shore), volcanoes are generally hazardous only to people close by.

Pyroclastic hazards come from a volcano's explosive activities. Pyroclastic flows are avalanches of very hot ash, rock, glass fragments, and gases blown out of vents. These materials can reach temperatures up to 1,500°F (815°C). Pyroclastic flows are also known as hot avalanches and *nuées ardentes* ("glowing clouds" in French). They move down a volcano's side between 100 and 150 miles (160 and 240 km) per hour. Due to their heat and speed, they are extremely dangerous. *Lateral blasts* are explosions of gas and ash from a volcano's side instead of its top. They flatten everything in their path. Ash falls result when an explosion from the volcano's crater sends millions of tons of ash into the atmosphere, where it is carried by the wind before dropping out. Ash falls may cover thousands of square miles of land.

Geologists (scientists who study Earth, its features, and its composition) use the Indonesian word *lahar* to refer to debris flows and mudflows. In both cases, large amounts of loose volcanic ash and small rocks move down the mountainside after mixing with water, sometimes at more than 40 miles (64 km) per hour. If over half of the material is larger than sand grains, a lahar is called a debris flow. If the particles are smaller than sand, it is called a mudflow. Because there is little warning, it is difficult to evacuate people from a lahar, which may reach down 50 miles (80 km) from a volcano's peak.

Lava flows look dangerous, but they are the least likely to kill people. Compared to pyroclastic flows and lahars, lava moves very slowly. The fastest lava flows move between 10 and 30 miles (16 and 48 km) per hour, but most move about 3.3 feet (1 m) per hour. Slower lava flows move only a few feet per day, so people can move out of the way. Buildings, of course, cannot move away, so they can catch fire from the heat.

Approximately 90 percent of the gas released from volcanoes is water vapor (steam). The rest includes carbon dioxide, carbon monoxide, and sulfur dioxide, which may be poisonous. Deaths from volcanic gases are extremely rare but may occur when these gases settle into low-lying areas and replace the air.

On August 17, 2002, Kilauea Volcano in Hawaii erupted, sending large surface flows of lava into the Pacific Ocean. Kilauea has been erupting intermittently for more than 20 years. (Photo courtesy of Associated Press)

Environmental Changes

Volcanoes are naturally occurring events—they are part of Earth's rock cycle that brings new rock to the surface while older rock is broken down by wind and water. So it is not really correct to say that volcanoes *damage* the environment instead; more accurately, volcanoes *change* the environment.

When a volcano spews out millions of tons of ash, much of it falls on or close to the mountain. The rest continues on, blown by the wind, for several thousand miles. The power of the eruption is sometimes so great that the ash enters the *stratosphere*—the atmospheric layer that starts between 6 and 10 miles (10 and 17 km) above Earth's surface. Large amounts of stratospheric ash may actually cool Earth for several months to a year or more by blocking the Sun's radiation. This causes a short-term climate change for the entire world.

Deep layers of ash (several feet or more) near the mountain, generally cover up all the plants. Some plants will die, but others have the ability to break through the ash and send their seeds out to reclaim the mountainside. Once the rainy season comes to the mountain, *erosion* will eat through the ash and allow more plants to take root. Areas away from the mountain will receive smaller amounts of ash, that—tilled into farmers' fields—will eventually make the soil more fertile and provide better crop yields.

Lahars and pyroclastic flows have a more dramatic effect over a smaller area than ash does. Due to the heat and amount of rocky material involved, these processes kill everything in their way and leave behind a deep path of rock and debris. In tropical areas, where moisture is abundant, seeds that blow in take root quickly among the rocks. Arriving insects make homes near the plants and birds and small mammals follow. Although the mountain and the vegetation and animals living around it will never look as they did before the eruption, nature has the remarkable ability to recover and exploit the newly created landscape to make it hospitable again.

Depending on a volcano's location and the type of eruption, it may be difficult for visitors to see signs of an eruption 50 to 100 years later. Once life starts to return, the recovery moves along at a faster rate. Within a short time, larger animals that make meals out of smaller ones move in. For nature, a volcanic eruption is not a disaster—it is just part of life.

Volcanoes as Disasters

Volcanoes are not disasters for nature, but they can be for people. USGS scientists estimate that worldwide, 500 million people living near tectonic plate boundaries could presently be in danger from volcanic eruptions. People who do not live near volcanoes may wonder why anyone would choose to live near a potentially dangerous mountain.

Volcanic areas can be attractive places to live. The soil surrounding volcanoes tends to be very fertile, because it contains many minerals that encourage plants to grow. Large numbers of plants encourage large numbers of animals. When ancient peoples lived by gathering and hunting food, volcanic areas provided everything they needed. Most people today eat food grown on farms, and the volcanic soil that provided a good environment for wild plants also provides a good environment for farmers' crops.

Volcanoes are potentially dangerous, but few volcanoes erupt often. People forget about the danger when hundreds or thousands of years pass between eruptions. A volcano is not very likely to erupt during a single lifetime. If people become convinced that a volcano will *never* erupt, they may build towns nearby. Some volcanic areas are not good places to live because the surrounding area is mountainous—the soil is rocky, and the terrain is steep— but they are great places to vacation, because nearby streams, lakes, and forests are wonderful spots for hiking, camping, and boating. Whether people live or play near a volcano, they could be in danger if it erupts. (The differences between active, dormant, and extinct volcanoes are discussed in the "Active, 'Sleeping,' or Totally Dead?" sidebar below.)

The United States is a geographically large country that has lots of open space where people may choose to live. Because of this, people who settle near volcanoes do so by choice. In countries like Japan, with small land areas, large populations, and several volcanoes, it is impossible for everyone to live a safe distance away from volcanoes. The danger to human life can be reduced, however, if people have safe places to go and enough warning to get there.

Unlike other natural disasters (hurricanes, tornadoes, floods, earthquakes) that may last a few minutes or a few days, volcanic

Active, "Sleeping," or Totally Dead?

Volcanoes are considered *active* if there is any kind of geologic activity associated with them. A volcano that just emits some steam (for example, Mount Baker in northern Washington) is still considered active. Other volcanoes are "sleeping" or *dormant*. These volcanoes are not currently active, but geologists think they could become active again because of their geologic features. For example, the volcano may be near an active tectonic plate boundary. Mount Shasta, in northern California, is a dormant volcano. Its last significant eruption occurred in 1786. The volcano emitted a few puffs of steam in 1855 but has been cooling steadily ever since.

Volcanoes that have not erupted in tens of thousands of years and are no longer near an area of seismic activity are considered "dead" or *extinct*. Geologists do not think that extinct volcanoes will ever become active in the future. An example of an extinct volcano is the Hawaiian island of Oahu. This volcano last erupted over 1 million years ago. Oahu has moved away from the hot spot that produced the island.

eruptions may rage on for months or years. People living near an erupting volcano may not have the option of rebuilding their homes and may need to move away.

Volcanoes in History

Each year, there are 50 to 60 volcanic eruptions around the world. Volcanic activity was reported at 52 different volcanoes during 2003—many of these produced multiple steam and ash plumes or lava flows. But eruptions are not memorable unless they cause many deaths and a lot of property damage. In the past 200 years, there have been a number of deadly volcanoes. The following examples are among the best-known volcanic eruptions.

The Krakatau volcano was in the Sunda Strait between the Indonesian islands of Java and Sumatra. Earthquakes had rocked the supposedly extinct Krakatau for about six years before it started erupting on May 20, 1883. After a month of volcanic activity, it started to quiet down, but by the middle of August, three vents were still spewing steam and ash into the air. These eruptions remained relatively small until August 26, when large pyroclastic flows started rushing down the volcano and continued for three days. When the magma that had filled the chambers beneath the volcano emptied, the crater floor fell. Krakatau disappeared below the ocean's surface. The collapsing volcano generated a tsunami that sent a wall of water 115 feet (35 m) high into the islands of Java and Sumatra. The eruption itself killed no one, but the high water wiped out 165 villages and their 36,000 residents.

Krakatau pumped so much ash into the atmosphere that it reduced the amount of sunlight that could reach Earth's surface. During 1884, the average global temperature dropped by 0.9°F (0.5°C). Five years passed before all of the ash fell to Earth and the climate returned to normal.

Mont Pelée, on the Caribbean island of Martinique, began erupting in late April 1902. At first, the eruption just produced a small cinder cone on the floor of the crater. In early May, a lake within the crater flowed out through a gap in the crater wall and fed mudflows that moved down the mountainside. After several days of mudflows, Mont Pelée exploded with a huge roar on the morning of May 8, sending a large ash cloud into the sky and a fiery *nuée ardente* down the side of the mountain toward the town of St. Pierre, 4 miles (6.4 km) away. (The "Plinian and Peléan Eruptions" sidebar on page 12 further discusses the differences between this type of eruption and that of volcanoes such as Krakatau.) The eruption left behind 1.6 feet (0.5 m) of ash and small bits of rock and killed more than 30,000 residents. The 1,300°F (700°C) gas and ash cloud set fires, knocked over stone walls, and even turned over ships that were anchored in the port.

A number of factors contributed to the Mont Pelée disaster. Although the volcano had been rumbling for a couple of months and a strong smell of sulfur (the "rotten egg" smell) was filling the town of St. Pierre, residents were told that lava from the volcano could never reach the town. Therefore, even though people had time to leave the island, few did. When the eruption occurred at 8 A.M. Atlantic Standard Time (AST), it took only five minutes for the pyroclastic flow to reach St. Pierre. The people who were not killed instantly died when the ash suffocated them.

Nevado del Ruiz in Colombia started erupting in November 1984 and continued to erupt every once in a while in 1985. On November 13, 1985, the volcano produced small ash deposits and pyroclastic flows. A major pyroclastic flow occurred around 9:00 P.M. Colombia Time (COT). The flow melted part of a glacier, creating some small lahars. The lahars grew faster and larger as they picked up more water and dirt. The largest lahar was 131 feet (40 m) deep and moving 19 to 25 miles (30 to 40 km) per hour when it struck the town of Armero, 44 miles (70 km) away from the volcano. The lahar killed almost 23,000 sleeping people, left another 10,000 homeless, and cost $7.7 billion in property damage.

The people of Armero did not have to die. Scientists knew that Armero was built on mudflows dating from an 1845 eruption. They warned that Armero was in the path of future lahars, but government officials did not make emergency evacuation plans. When Nevado del Ruiz started its major eruption, scientists advised emergency personnel to evacuate Armero and nearby towns. Government officials did tell Armero police that the town was in danger, but no one made the decision to evacuate.

The disaster in Armero was on the minds of Philippine geologists when Mount Pinatubo woke up after a 400-year nap on April 2, 1991. The first part of the eruption consisted of steam explosions followed by thick ash. Geologists at the Philippine Institute of Volcanology and Seismology quickly placed a *seismograph* (a device for measuring the strength of earthquakes) at a spot 5 miles (8 km) west of the volcano. Within 24 hours, the device had measured over 200 small earthquakes.

In Armero, Colombia, the volcano Nevado del Ruiz erupted in 1985, killing more than 20,000 people in the town surrounding the mountain. A few people survived despite the government's failure to evacuate the town of Armero. (Photo courtesy of Associated Press)

Government officials evacuated everyone who lived within 6.2 miles (10 km) of the volcano. The geologists installed more seismographs all around the mountain and recorded even more earthquakes. But there was just too much information coming in from the instruments—geologists were having a difficult time processing all of it. A special team from the USGS flew in to set up a center for analyzing and processing the data from the network of seismic sensors. This team helped prepare hazard maps that showed who was in danger. As they examined the geologic landforms around the volcano, they discovered that Clark Air Force Base was sitting on top of pyroclastic flows that had been deposited from previous eruptions 600, 2,500, and 4,600 years before. The area around the base was in serious danger.

Scientists started briefing government leaders and local residents about Pinatubo's possible dangers, including pyroclastic

Plinian and Pelean Eruptions

Eruptions like those of Krakatau are called *Plinian eruptions* because they were first described by the scholar Pliny the Younger in A.D. 79, when Mount Vesuvius in Italy erupted. Such eruptions consist of continuous, powerful gas explosions that throw out very large amounts of *pumice* (glassy lava full of air bubbles). Some eruptions start with a short blast of gas and rock, followed by oozing lava. Others shoot out gas and rock continuously and may also produce a *nuée ardente*. The first blast may send smaller ash and rock particles out for many miles, but if the eruption continues over a long period, larger chunks of rock will be thrown from the crater and land on the sides of the volcano.

Pelean eruptions, named after the eruption of Mont Pelée, produce thick magmas, *nuées ardentes*, and smaller ash falls than other volcanoes. Until the eruption of Mont Pelée, geologists were unaware of the dangers of pyroclastic flows.

flows and lahars. They also created a warning system that started with 0 (no alert) and went up to 5 (volcano erupting). By June 9, 1991, the scientists had moved the alert level up to 5—Pinatubo was going to explode. Approximately 50,000 people within 12.4 miles (20 km) of the mountain evacuated. The main eruption started on June 12 as an ash column reached a height of 14.9 miles (24 km). Officials then evacuated everyone within 18.6 miles (30 km) of the volcano as pyroclastic flows moved 3.7 miles (6 km) down the mountain from the peak. The largest eruption occurred on June 15, when the ash cloud reached a height of 25 miles (40 km) and the pyroclastic flows covered 29 square miles (75 km²)—the entire area that had been identified as being in danger.

The volcanic eruption may have been over, but the dangers were not. A typhoon (hurricane) hit the area, dropping over 10 inches (25.4 cm) of rain. The rain mixed with the loose ash and debris on the mountainside, and lahars swept down into the valleys below. Two hundred thousand more people fled as the wall of water and mud flowed over their homes. Because of the advance preparations, Mount Pinatubo's eruptions killed no one, but illnesses and roof collapses as a result of the event did kill approximately 300 people living in refugee camps. (Lahars continue to be a problem because of the massive amount of loose ash that remains. The Philippines receives large amounts of rain, and when it mixes with the ash, the mud comes down the mountain.)

Massive loss of life due to eruptions has been reduced due to advanced warning efforts such as those seen during the Mount Pinatubo eruptions. But volcanoes remain dangerous. Two Indonesian volcanoes, Mount Bromo and Mount Awu, erupted within two days of each other in June 2004, spewing large rocks and ash into the air. Two tourists died from Bromo's eruption while they were hiking in a nearby national park. Both Bromo and Awu have been active volcanoes since the early 18th century, and Awu has killed more than 8,000 people since 1711.

CHAPTER 2

Mount St. Helens Roars to Life

The Toutle River, north of Kelso, Washington, filled with volcanic mud as a result of the explosion of Mount St. Helens on May 18, 1980. (Photo courtesy of CORBIS)

Mount St. Helens is one of 14 volcanoes in the Cascade Range, a mountain chain that stretches from British Columbia to northern California. Before the eruption of 1980, Mount St. Helens was a magnificent, almost perfectly symmetrical peak soaring 9,677 feet (2,950 m) into the often-cloudy skies of western Washington. Mount St. Helens was often compared to Japan's famous Fujiyama, because they shared the same type of majestic profile. *Loo-wit*—"mountain given special beauty by the Great Spirit"— was one of the names given to it by the Native Americans of the Klickitat tribe. Dense forests around the mountain were home to

a wide variety of wildlife. Mount St. Helens was part of the Gifford Pinchot National Forest. Hundreds of thousands of people each year enjoyed camping, hiking, and fishing near the mountain. Small farms dotted the surrounding valleys.

The local economy depended upon these vacationers and on logging. The timber industry employed several thousand people to harvest wood and mill it into lumber for building. The economic strength of the area depended upon the demand for lumber. When it was high, the people prospered.

The three counties that surrounded Mount St. Helens—Cowlitz, Lewis, and Skamania—had a total of 144,000 people at the time of the blast. The mountain towns closest to the volcano were very small—usually 1,500 people or less. About 45,000 people lived within the floodplains of the rivers that cut through the area.

Why Study Mount St. Helens?

Volcanoes rarely erupt in the continental United States (the 48 states not including Hawaii and Alaska). Mount St. Helens was the first volcano to erupt in the continental U.S. in almost 60 years (Mount Lassen in California stopped erupting in 1921), and it produced the largest landslide in recorded history—3.7 billion cubic yards (2.8 billion m³), or about three wheelbarrows full of debris for everyone in the world. The eruption was a spectacular explosion that allowed geologists a firsthand look at volcanic behavior. Because of its location and unique behavior, Mount St. Helens has become the most studied volcano in history.

Mount St. Helens is also important to study because humans have not interfered with the devastation that the volcano left behind. With the creation of the Mount St. Helens National Volcanic Monument, the recovery has been left up to nature. The monument has become a natural laboratory that lets scientists study how life develops. For more information on this natural laboratory, see Chapters 6 and 7.

Mount St. Helens is an important lesson in what can go wrong when people respond to a natural disaster. Communication and coordination are key ingredients in a successful response. Both were missing in the aftermath of one of the major eruptions of the 20th century.

The Eruption of Mount St. Helens

Mount St. Helens has erupted many times. Since the last eruption in 1857, thousands of people moved near the mountain. Towns sprang up along the rivers that were fed by mountain snow. Townspeople lived right in the path of mudflows and floods that an eruption would produce. The mountain's previous eruption is highlighted in the "Last Eruptive Period" sidebar on the following page.

Three factors contributed to the extent of the human disaster caused by Mount St. Helens in 1980. First, many people thought that the volcano would not erupt. Earthquakes were the first signs that the volcano was coming back to life. However, the Cascade Range, of which Mount St. Helens is just one mountain, quakes on a regular basis. Any area that is near a tectonic plate boundary—including the west coast of the United States—is prone to earthquakes. So most people just shrugged off the suggestion that the earthquakes could be a sign of upcoming volcanic activity. Furthermore, because there had not been a major eruption of the volcano in almost 150 years, people assumed that it would not erupt again, and they ignored warnings to stay away from it.

Second, because the national forest surrounding the mountain was so important to the local economy—both for business and recreational use—people were reluctant to take steps that could potentially save lives if the volcano did erupt. Weyerhaeuser—a major timber company and employer in the Mount St. Helens area—stood to lose millions of dollars if it could not harvest trees from its land near the volcano. Without the trees, the company's employees would have no work. If Weyerhaeuser employees had no incomes, then local businesses that sold them goods and services would likewise have been in serious financial trouble. Gifford Pinchot National Forest, surrounding the volcano, is an important recreation area. Tens of thousands of people, most of them from Washington and Oregon, enjoy using the forest each year. Government officials could have kept everyone out of the area, but that would have caused economic hardship there.

Third, because there was a lot of snow and ice on the mountain when it erupted, the rapidly melting water and the full rivers and streams increased the extent of the mud-flows, and they reached all the way to the Columbia River. Under any circumstances, as hot magma moved toward the surface of the mountain, it could have triggered huge avalanches of snow and ice, sending rapidly melting water into streams and rivers and flooding low-lying areas. But because the eruption took place before the summer melt, the additional snow and ice mixed with the hot rock, ash, and debris to extend the mud-flows farther down the mountain and into the valleys below. This created the sedimentation problems that plagued the Columbia River for the next several years.

The Last Eruptive Period

The Pacific Northwest's native peoples—including the Klickitat, Coast Salish, Cowlitz, and Spokane tribes—were the only witnesses to Mount St. Helens's eruptions in the early 19th century. When the mountain started erupting in 1831, it entered a 26-year period of volcanic activity. Based on witnesses' reports—including those of missionaries J.L. Parrish and Samuel Parker, and Dr. Meredith Gairdner, physician for the Hudson Bay Company at Fort Vancouver, Washington—and the geological evidence, there were probably major eruptions between 1831 and 1835, and in 1842 and 1843. Plumes of ash and steam were the most common form of activity, although there were some lava flows and mudflows. There are no records of any deaths or injuries due to these events.

Warnings and Preparation

Mount St. Helens ended its slumber when an earthquake with a magnitude of 4.2 on the *Richter scale* rocked the mountain on March 20, 1980. (The Richter scale is a numerical scale used to describe the amount of shaking during an earthquake.) Within two days, the number of quakes increased, and the *epicenter* (the point at which the earthquake takes place) appeared to be rising within the mountain toward the surface. By March 24, seismographs were recording up to 20 earthquakes per hour—one reached 4.7 on the Richter scale. That prompted University of Washington *seismologist* (earthquake specialist) Steve Malone to call the USGS office in Denver, Colorado. "There is something significant going on at St. Helens," he told the USGS. Within a few days, geologists from all over the United States had converged on Mount St. Helens with special monitoring equipment.

As geologists placed their equipment on the mountain, USGS and state officials met to discuss the possibility of an eruption. U.S. Forest Service (USFS) officials who managed the Gifford Pinchot National Forest surrounding Mount St. Helens decided to keep people away from the peak. They also suggested that visitors not

A cloud of steam rises from Mount St. Helens, carrying ash that would spread across the United States within days. (Photo courtesy of U.S. Geological Survey)

spend nights on the mountain, because it would be too difficult to rescue them from an avalanche or eruption in the dark.

Two days later, on March 27, steam and ash punched out of a new crater 200 feet (61 m) in diameter and 150 feet (46 m) deep. Geologists monitoring the mountain's condition saw several new cracks—some almost 3 miles (4.8 km) long.

First the Ash, Then a Bulge

By the middle of April, a bulge on the north flank of the mountain was 1.5 miles (2.4 km) in diameter and rapidly filling with magma. USGS geologists measured the size of the bulge daily by bouncing laser beams off it. Some areas had grown 450 feet (137 km) higher in just a few weeks. The worried USGS geologists issued a hazard alert on April 30, advising emergency personnel that the bulge was "the most serious potential hazard posed by the current volcanic activity at Mount St. Helens." If the bulge continued to grow, it could send ice and snow down the mountain in a spectacular avalanche.

Monitors on the mountain were recording *harmonic tremors* (continuous, rhythmic shaking), which indicated that magma was starting to move beneath Earth's surface. USGS geologists, realizing the potential eruptive power of the volcano, briefed newspaper and television reporters. Geologist David Johnston gave his blunt assessment while standing just a few miles from the mountain: "This is like standing next to a dynamite keg," he said, "and the fuse is lit, but you don't know how long the fuse is. If it [Mount St. Helens] exploded [right now], we would die."

By April 8, the new crater was 1,700 feet (520 m) across and 850 feet (260 m) deep. To keep people a safe distance away, local officials set up road barriers. The volcano took a little break in late April and into early May. No more steam and ash puffed out. People who did not believe the volcano would erupt were even more convinced that they were right. They thought that geologists and emergency officials were just trying to scare them.

The Landslide

"Vancouver, Vancouver. This is it!" These were the last words of Johnston, monitoring the volcano from Coldwater Ridge just 6 miles (9.6 km) away. He was reporting to his colleagues stationed in Vancouver, Washington, a city on the Columbia River. Seconds later, he was blown away by the force of the eruption. (The "Excitement in the Air" sidebar on the following page tells more about the very first announcement of the eruption, which occurred on public radio.) The eruption was not just one event—it was actually several individual events spread over 10 hours. Each represented a different volcanic hazard and changed the landscape in its own way.

At 8:32 A.M. Pacific Daylight Time (PDT) on Sunday, May 18, 1980, a 5.1 earthquake struck the mountain. The bulge disappeared. The north face of the mountain started to shake, the ground rippled, and the entire north half of Mount St. Helens, with its load of snow, ice, and trees, slid downhill at 155 to 180 miles (250 to 290 km) per hour. This was the largest avalanche in recorded history. Sliding across the western part of Spirit Lake, the avalanche landed against a ridge 1,200 feet (365 m) high some 6 miles (9.6 km) to the north of the mountain and pushed over the top. When part of the water that was pushed out of Spirit Lake flowed back down the ridge and into the lakebed, it brought hundreds of dead trees with it.

The Lateral Blast

Lateral blasts are very rare. Most eruptions occur through the vent at the top of the mountain because it is the weakest spot. The only previously known sideways blast occurred in 1956, during an eruption of Bezymianny, a volcano on the Kamchatka Peninsula of Russia. Scientists are now looking at the geologic evidence left behind from older eruptions to see if lateral blasts are perhaps more common than they are believed to be.

Excitement in the Air

The first person to announce the eruption of Mount St. Helens was Mike Beard, a reporter for radio station KGW in Portland, Oregon. Flying near Mount St. Helens, Beard exclaimed to his astonished listeners, "There's smoke and ashes pouring out of it! There is no doubt the eruption is starting." Upon hearing this report, workers at the Washington Department of Emergency Services (DES) unsuccessfully tried to call the radio station to confirm the eruption. Totally frustrated at their inability to get a phone call through, they called their associates at Oregon's Emergency Services Division and asked them to call KGW. Once the eruption was confirmed, they passed the information to Washington's governor, Dixy Lee Ray.

Ray was speaking to a group of Washington superior court judges. Enthusiastic about the possibility of a full eruption, Ray said, "I've always said, for many years, that I hoped I lived long enough to see one of our volcanoes erupt. Maybe soon I will get a chance." Upon leaving the meeting, Ray boarded an airplane for an aerial look at Mount St. Helens.

At Mount St. Helens, the weight of the ice and rock on the mountainside had forced gases to stay within the magma beneath it. After the landslide, the pressure was released, and the gas exploded out. Hot steam, rock, ash, and glacial ice shot straight out and then down the mountainside—much more dangerous than if they had gone straight up. The sound of the explosion is discussed in the "Big Boom" sidebar on page 22.

With an estimated temperature as high as 600°F (315°C), the flow of hot ash and rock had a starting speed of 220 miles (355 km) per hour. Toward the bottom of the mountain, it was moving at almost the speed of sound—730 miles (1,175 km) per hour. The flow very quickly overtook the avalanche. The hot ash and rock moved 19 miles (31 km) north of the crater over a width of 23 miles (37 km), leaving a fan-shaped path of destruction more than three times the size of the District of Columbia. Everything in the way was reduced to small bits, blown down, or burned up.

Within an 8-mile (12.9-km) radius of the crater, known as the "Blast Zone," not even the soil was left. Only bare bedrock remained. Moving away from the crater, the next area was the "Blow-down Zone," where the trees were flash burned and blown over. Only the trunks were left and they were laid flat, like giant black toothpicks, pointing in the direction of the hurricane-force winds that had swirled around them. Beyond this zone, about 14 to 17 miles (23 to 27 km) from the crater, was the "Scorch Zone." In this area, heat killed the trees, but there was not enough explosive energy to blow them over.

Pyroclastic Flows and Lahars

With temperatures of at least 1,300°F (705°C) and moving at 50 to 80 miles (80 to 130 km) per hour, scorching pyroclastic flows reached 5 miles (8 km) north of the crater. These flows consisted of extremely bright, hot pumice. Each flow left behind pumice to a depth of between 3 and 30 feet (0.9 and 9 meters)—though in some areas, pumice was over 120 feet (37 m) deep, and in one spot, it was 300 feet (91 m) deep.

Three events contributed to the mudflows after the eruption. When the north flank of the mountain collapsed, it squeezed water out of very small openings in the rocks, which mixed with the landslide, moving it faster. The pyroclastic flows melted snow and ice that added more water to the lahars. Other pyroclastic flows entered lakes

The Big Boom

Which people heard a large explosion when the first blast exploded out of the north side of Mount St. Helens—those a few miles away or those a couple of hundred miles away? Actually, the people close by heard nothing. An atmospheric condition called an *inversion* (when air temperature increases with height instead of decreasing, as it normally does) was in place. Inversions often occur when the wind brings warm air into an area that is very cold. Cold air is heavier than warm air, so the cold air hugs the ground, while the warm air sits on top of it. The layer of warm air acts much like a lid placed on top of a container, trapping sound waves that hit it and reflecting them back toward the ground. As the sound traveled up from the peak, this "cap" of warm air bent the sound down toward distant points. The people in Vancouver, British Columbia—some 225 miles (360 km) away—heard the building-shaking blast.

and streams, mixed with the water, and made a thick mud that continued downstream.

The mudflows struck the rivers closest to the mountain at 8:35 A.M. (PDT). As the water raced down the mountainside, it picked up ash, rock, trees—whatever was in its path—and carried them at speeds of up to 80 miles (130 km) per hour. By 10:00 A.M. (PDT), a 12-foot (3.7-m) wall of water, mud, and debris had reached 27 miles (43 km) from the crater. By noon, the mudflow was approaching the Cowlitz River—45 miles (72 km) away from the crater. The mud was so hot that it raised the river's normal temperature of about 40°F (4°C) to 90°F (32°C). Salmon leaped out of the river to avoid the hot mud. When the mudflow stopped, the Cowlitz could carry only 15 percent of the water that it had carried before the eruption due to the deposits of sediment. Leaving the Cowlitz and plunging into the Columbia River, the sediment left the Columbia at one-third of its previous depth.

A second, larger mudflow moved down the North Fork of the Toutle River in the afternoon. At 2:30 P.M. (PDT), it wiped out a Weyerhaeuser logging camp. As it continued downstream, the mudflow picked up more logs. They worked like battering rams as they hit the bridges that spanned the North Fork. Seven bridges were destroyed.

Ash Falls

At 8:47 A.M. (PDT), the top 1,300 feet (400 m) of Mount St. Helens blew off, sending a cloud of rock and ash into the sky. The plume could be seen for hundreds of miles. The cloud carried 1.4 billion cubic yards (1.1 billion m³) of ash into the atmosphere, where it reached a height of 80,000 feet (24,400 m) in less than 15 minutes. As the eruption continued over the next nine hours, the larger, heavier particles fell out first, close to the mountain. The wind carried smaller particles into Idaho and Montana. On a day that became known as "Ash Sunday," the ash cloud plunged the cities of

Yakima, 90 miles (145 km) to the east, and Spokane, 300 miles (480 km) to the east, into darkness. Within three days, the ash had spread across the United States. The ash that penetrated the stratosphere—approximately 6.8 miles (11 km) above Earth—took 15 days to circle the entire planet.

On June 30, 1980, the western side of Mount St. Helens can be seen over the Toutle River, which is filled with volcanic mud. The landscape is barren due to the May eruption. (Photo courtesy of Associated Press)

Continuing Eruptions

On May 25, Mount St. Helens erupted again, sending an ash cloud up to 9 miles (14.5 km) into the air and pyroclastic flows down the north flank of the volcano. This time the winds were blowing toward the west, so southwestern Washington and northwestern Oregon received the ash.

The next eruption occurred on June 12, when ash and steam pushed 7 miles (11.3 km) into the atmosphere, and pyroclastic flows 6 to 12 feet (1.8 to 3.7 m) deep headed into Spirit Lake. The wind carried the ash cloud over Vancouver, Washington, and Portland, Oregon, and continued on to the Oregon coast. The next day, a lava *dome*—composed of extremely slow-moving lava—formed in the crater. The mound of cracked and broken lava was 130 feet (40 m) high and 1,000 feet (305 m) across.

Additional eruptions occurred on July 22, August 7, and October 16 to 18. The July and August eruptions sent up ash clouds and produced more pyroclastic flows. They also destroyed the previous domes inside the crater and created new ones. The October eruptions produced several small pyroclastic flows, destroyed the dome created on August 7, and then created yet another dome. That dome has remained in the crater, continuing to grow larger. In 2000 the dome stood 876 feet (267 m) above the crater floor and was 3,500 feet (1,070 m) in diameter.

Loss of Life

County and state authorities had a difficult time determining exactly how many people died during the eruption of Mount St. Helens. Areas close to the mountain had been blasted down to bare rock, and no bodies were left behind. Nine people were confirmed dead on the day of the blast—either because they were known to be in the Blast Zone or because their bodies were found farther away from the mountain. After two years, the official number of dead and missing (presumed dead) stood at 57. Twenty-seven of the bodies were never found. Almost everyone died within a few minutes due to suffocation by the ash. Some died of burns after walking out of the region affected by the eruption. All had been in "safe" areas.

Swarms, Ash, and Glowing Lava

With the exception of two short earthquake events in 1998 and 2001, Mount St. Helens entered a quiet phase after October 1986. Then on September 23, 2004, earthquake *swarms* again shook the mountain. (When earthquakes are so numerous that they occur at the rate of hundreds in a day, they are termed swarms by geoscientists.) The 200 quakes were all less than magnitude 1. Several days later, more swarms occurred in which the intensity increased to between magnitude 2 and 2.8. Scientists at the Cascade Volcano Observatory issued a "Notice of Volcanic Unrest," cautioning people in the area that the volcano was becoming active again.

By September 29, seismic activity had increased, and the observatory issued an alert which signified that an eruption might occur. By the next day, the National Weather Service had started issuing fallout advisories so people living downwind from the volcano would be prepared for ash falls.

At noon on October 1, an ash and steam cloud billowed 10,000 feet (3,050 m) into the air. By 2 P.M. (PDT), continuous, low-frequency tremors indicated that magma was moving up through the mountain. Steam and ash emissions continued periodically through October 5, and towns within 30 miles (48 km) of the volcano received light dustings of ash. A lessening of seismic activity occurred on October 6, but scientists continued to closely monitor the area. The dome within the crater was beginning to bulge, the result of 70.7 cubic feet (2 million m³) of magma pushing up each day.

A week later, on October 13, a new lobe of lava appeared at the surface, forming a "fin" some 200 feet (61 m) long and 60 feet (18 m) high. As the lava oozed onto the surface, jets of ash-filled steam shot up tens of meters within the crater. As night fell, scientists flying overhead could see the lava glowing eerily below them. Mount St. Helens let volcanologists know that she was not yet ready to "sleep."

CHAPTER 3

The Response

Local, state, and federal agencies all began to prepare for an eruption as the earthquake swarms under Mount St. Helens intensified in May 1980. However, the agencies were not really prepared to handle a natural disaster. They did not successfully coordinate their efforts before the May 18 eruption. As a result, the response was well intended but not as effective as it could—or should—have been.

In Oregon, a bus driver cleans ash from his windshield after the May 18 explosion of Mount St. Helens. (Photo courtesy of Annie Griffiths Belt/CORBIS)

Local and State Government Preparations

After the March 27 eruption, county emergency officials started evacuating residents, including eight residents of the Lewis River valley and 100 residents who lived near the North and South Forks of the Toutle River. An eruption could rapidly melt the mountain's snow and ice, sending floodwaters sweeping through people's homes. Possible flooding also led Weyerhaeuser to move 300 of its workers from a logging camp. The 20 employees of the Toutle River Hatchery—a salmon *hatchery*—also evacuated.

The Cowlitz and Skamania county sheriffs wanted to keep people a safe distance from the volcano, so they ordered their deputies to put up roadblocks. This effort was largely unsuccessful because there were too many ways to enter the forest surrounding Mount St. Helens other than the paved roads. There

Although initially unprepared for a natural disaster like the eruption of Mount St. Helens, Washington governor Dixy Lee Ray mobilized government agencies to take measures to keep people safe immediately following the eruptions in early May. Unfortunately, all plans were not in place when the most damaging explosion occurred on May 18, 1980. (Photo courtesy of Wally McNamee/ CORBIS)

were 3,700 miles (5,940 km) of logging roads and hundreds of miles of trails leading into the mountain. Some people familiar with the area knew how to hike in without using trails. As frustrated Skamania County sheriff William Closner said, "People went over, under, through, and around [roadblocks] every time we tried to restrict access to what we believed were dangerous areas." Closner had found people selling maps that showed how to evade the roadblocks. "People were climbing right up to the rim of the crater," Closner continued. "It would have taken the U.S. Army to control those people."

The sheriff's office quickly assembled a pamphlet describing the major dangers from an eruption—ash fall and flooding. The sheriff's office also developed a system to warn residents to evacuate and told residents how to protect themselves and prepare for an evacuation. In the city of Toutle, the school district created a plan to shelter students in case the volcano erupted during school hours.

Unfortunately for the state of Washington, its Department of Emergency Services (DES) was prepared for a military attack but totally unprepared for a natural disaster. The recently created Federal Emergency Management Agency (FEMA), which itself had difficulty handling natural disasters, had ranked Washington's DES "at or near the bottom" of all state disaster agencies. Responding to this stinging criticism, Governor Dixy Lee Ray appointed restaurant owner and former campaign worker Edward Chow Jr. to take over the DES. Chow's job was to fix the agency, even though he had no prior experience in disaster response. He took over in December 1979—just three months before the first eruption.

Washington's governor did not wait long after the eruption to take measures to keep people safe. On April 2, Governor Ray gathered important state agency heads to form the Mount St. Helens Watch Group. The next day, she declared a state of emergency, giving herself the authority to call on the National Guard for assistance. "Volcanic activity at Mount St. Helens has created conditions that may threaten life," Ray wrote, "and may result in widespread damage or destruction to private and public property in the state of Washington. I find that an emergency affecting life, health, and property exists within the state of Washington."

Ray ordered roadblocks to be moved farther away from the mountain. Tourists were discouraged from coming to the area. Ray also announced that the DES would be in charge of coordinating the efforts of all state agencies. This decision did not please people who considered the DES an extremely weak, ineffective organization. When DES director Chow told Ray that some agencies were opposed to his leadership, an enraged Ray pounded her fist and told Chow, "You're in charge!"

At the end of April, USFS and law enforcement personnel asked Governor Ray to establish a "Red Zone" that would extend from the mountain out 20 miles (32 km) in all directions. Such a zone would give officials legal grounds to keep people out of the dangerous area. When the Red Zone was finally established, however, it stopped where private timberland started. As a result, the western edge of the Red Zone was at most 3.6 miles (5.8 km) from the summit. The northern edge was 14 miles (22.5 km) from the peak, the eastern edge was 8 miles (12.9 km) away, and the southern edge was 6 miles (9.6 km) away. Timber companies could continue their logging activities.

Mount St. Helens's rumblings had stopped being front-page news in early May. That changed on May 9, when a strong earthquake shook the area. The DES asked Cowlitz and Skamania county officials to send in copies of their disaster plans. The state wanted to know how many people lived close to the mountain and how the state could assist in the event of an eruption. The disaster plans were due on May 19.

Also during early May, law enforcement and USFS personnel asked the DES to increase the size of the Red Zone. The DES did so, and it sent the new Red Zone map to Governor Ray's office for approval on May 17. That day, people living on Spirit Lake protested the barricading of the area (see the "Protesting the Barricades" sidebar below). The new Red Zone map was still sitting on the governor's desk the next day when Mount St. Helens exploded.

Federal Government Preparations

As Mount St. Helens continued to shake, the USGS and the USFS both took action to keep government agencies and the general public advised of the volcano's status. USGS geologists gave pamphlets to public officials, newspapers, and television and radio stations that described what to do if the volcano erupted. They also met with residents to provide current information about the volcano threat.

The USFS gave sightseers flyers warning of the danger. The service also called a meeting for March 26 to plan for a major eruption, inviting geologists, landowners, and representatives of county and state emergency agencies to attend. As the meeting ended, Ben Bena of the Cowlitz County Sheriff's Department

Protesting the Barricades

People who owned cabins near Spirit Lake were upset that they were being kept away from their property—which was within the Red Zone. They decided to hold a protest at the barricade blocking them from the Spirit Lake Highway. There were rumors that some of them intended to bring rifles and force their way past law enforcement personnel guarding the highway. Governor Ray agreed to allow residents desiring to bring out their personal property to do so *if* they signed a form saying that the state of Washington was not responsible for their safety. On Saturday, May 17, about 20 families drove to Spirit Lake with police leading the way. As the caravan of cars snaked up the mountain, State Patrol Chief Robert Landon expressed the heartfelt wish of everyone involved: "We hope the good Lord will keep that mountain from giving us any trouble." The families, loaded down with belongings, left Spirit Lake late that afternoon. The next day, another 20 families had permission to drive up the mountain. The volcano erupted early in the morning before they started.

demanded to know, "Who's going to be in charge? If the mountain blows, who is going to take control?" He did not get an answer. The USFS announced that it would form an Emergency Coordination Center to provide information to both government agencies and private industries. The service also developed an emergency plan for an eruption, but the plan only contained the names and phone numbers of people to contact—therefore, it was not much of a plan. Bena and the sheriff's department decided to develop their own emergency plan.

The next day, March 27, smoke and ash poured out from Mount St. Helens. Kurt Austermann of the USFS said, "We don't want to unjustly panic anybody, but we don't want to give them undue reassurances, either." The hope of keeping people informed without alarming them led some residents to believe that there was no serious danger from the volcano.

Before the major eruption of May 18, no agency was yet responsible for coordinating the response to the disaster. There was no final emergency plan that involved all the agencies. There was no search-and-rescue plan to aid people trapped on the mountain or by floods. There was no complete plan for restricting access to areas that might be affected by an eruption. Finally, there was no plan for evacuating Weyerhaeuser's 1,000 employees who worked within a few miles of the mountain. This lack of advanced planning would create problems in the hours and days that followed the big eruption.

Local and State Officials— Sheriffs Take Charge

The May 18 eruption was far more extensive than anyone had expected. The lack of coordination and of an active central communications center slowed the response. Although plans had been previously made for a communications center, it was not sufficient to deal with the emergency.

As the volcano erupted, Cowlitz County deputies acted on their emergency plan. Sirens blaring, they drove on prearranged routes through valleys, telling people to evacuate. They called volunteers living in flood-prone areas who told their neighbors. Radio stations carried emergency information. All the residents in the flood area were able to escape before water and mud filled their homes and farms. The fire department manned the roadblocks. Almost all of Toutle's residents evacuated, particularly after they heard that a poisonous gas cloud was approaching. There was no gas cloud, but the rumor may have aided in getting people to safety quickly.

Once the initial evacuations were complete, local officials started receiving dozens of calls from the families and friends of those who had been near Mount St. Helens. But no one had the responsibility of collecting information on missing persons or providing information to their families, so the families had a difficult time getting information. Although family and friends were the most likely to know just where the missing person was, federal regulations prevented family members from riding in helicopters and guiding the search-and-rescue crews. After the eruption, it was difficult to put rescue efforts under the control of one office. Each group—the sheriff's office, the National Guard, and the reserve squadrons flying the searches—wanted to be in control. As a result, no one was in control.

This situation changed on Tuesday night, May 20. The sheriffs from Lewis, Cowlitz, and Skamania counties split up the responsibilities. Lewis would coordinate ground searches, Cowlitz would coordinate air search-and-rescue efforts, and Skamania would be responsible for identifying the dead and putting together a list of those missing. In addition, officials from the three counties set up a central command post in the town of Toledo, 35 miles (56 km) northwest of Mount St. Helens. About 1,700 active duty and reserve soldiers who had been brought in to recover bodies, refuel aircraft, and provide maintenance joined the sheriffs' departments. Most of the disaster response came from county officials, and military reservists performed much of the search-and-rescue work. Governor Ray immediately requested federal funds to help with the disaster. Washington senator Warren Magnuson aided the governor by quickly pushing a $1 billion relief bill through Congress.

A year after the eruption, however, less than half the money had been spent. State officials were having a difficult time deciding what to do with it. The Small Business Administration (SBA) was aiding small businesses; FEMA was supporting part of the cleanup; and the Army Corps of Engineers was funding the river dredging and flood-control projects. Once the obvious needs—cleaning up ash and rebuilding roads and bridges—had been taken care of, it was less clear how the money could be effectively spent. So while state and local officials argued over how best to use the money, it remained unspent.

Federal Agencies—Search and Rescue

The morning of the eruption, Washington's Army National Guard and the U.S. Air Force Reserve's 304th Aerospace Rescue and Recovery Squadron both had helicopters in the air. Because no one was in charge of emergency response, no one had the authority to call in these search-and-rescue crews.

At 10:00 A.M. (PDT), approximately 90 minutes after the eruption started, the 304th received orders to head to Mount St. Helens. Normally, there would have been only 10 reservists on duty, but a training exercise was going on at Mount Hood, just 65 miles (105 km) south of the volcano, so 50 men were in uniform, ready to go. By noon, seven helicopter rescue crews were either at Mount St. Helens or on their way. The first two helicopters landed in Toutle. The pilots asked the National Guard troops standing by who was in charge. "No one yet," they responded. Pilot Mike Peters said, "Okay, then. I'm in charge." He divided the area into eight search sections and took off. As the helicopters got closer to

the mountain, the air became hazy, and the crews started to choke on the sulfur fumes. Within minutes, the pilots could hardly see where they were flying. As they rounded a hill, one of the crewmen pointed to flattened trees and exclaimed, "Look at that! What the heck happened?" Seeing no survivors, they continued on to Coldwater Ridge and found just bare rock.

Trees left behind by fast-moving mudflows surround a home downstream from Mount St. Helens. (Photo courtesy of U.S. Geological Survey)

After four hours in the air, the helicopters were headed for Kelso—home of the Cowlitz County Sheriff's Department—hoping to get gas. There, they met the deputies, National Guard troops, and Washington state troopers. Peters told them that no one could possibly be alive in the region affected by the blast.

As it turned out, Peters was incorrect. There were survivors trying to make their way to safety. Seven of the 304th's helicopters flew all day, rescuing 55 people from the flooding and mudflows.

The 116th Armored Cavalry, Washington Army National Guard, in Yakima—90 miles (145 km) away—was also ready to move. The troops had been asked to accompany the people who were planning to drive to Spirit Lake later that morning. The helicopter crews were going to fly above the people in their cars. In an emergency, they could quickly land, rescue the people, and fly them out. They did not know that Mount St. Helens had erupted until they saw what looked like a line of thunderstorms moving their way at 10:00 A.M. (PDT). The "thunderstorms" were actually large ash clouds. Because the troops delayed their takeoff, only 20 of their 32 helicopters could get off the ground due to the heavy ash fall. Landing in Kelso at noon, the crews decided to join in the rescue of people who might be caught in the floods and mudflows.

As darkness fell, the pilots had to stop searching. There was still no coordination among the search-and-rescue teams. No one group of people knew who was missing, who had been found and where, or what areas surrounding the mountain had been searched. No one was giving pilots information on where to fly, so they just decided on their own. This led to duplication of effort—flight crews were going over the same areas instead of searching new ones. All the ash on the ground hampered the ground search teams—not even four-wheel-drive vehicles worked.

By Monday, there were so many helicopters in the air that the chance of a midair collision was rapidly increasing. A communications plane flew in from March Air Force Base in California to provide air traffic control near the mountain. By Tuesday, the helicopter crews had found all the survivors. Now the bodies of the dead needed to be removed, but it took two more days before the crews received permission from their superiors to fly the recovery missions.

FEMA provided $86 million for cleaning up the ash, but much of it went unclaimed. Under FEMA rules, cities like Yakima, for example, that faced "ash drifts" up to 5 feet (1.5 m) high, could use the funds to buy brooms, but not shovels. The brooms were almost useless, while the shovels were what the cleanup teams needed. Since the money could not be used in ways that benefited towns and cities, only one-third of the money was spent.

The SBA also set aside $430 million to provide loans to businesses harmed by the eruption. Unfortunately, once business owners filled out the necessary forms, it took the SBA more than six months to process them. A year after the eruption, only $68 million had been given out. The laws under which the SBA worked could not be adapted to a volcanic disaster, and many people who would have been eligible had the damage been caused by a flood, tornado, or hurricane were unable to receive loans.

The Public Response to Danger

The people who lived near Mount St. Helens—like many who live near quiet volcanoes—did not believe that it was a hazard. Those who thought it might erupt did not think an eruption would harm them or damage their property. This belief continued after the March 27 eruption. Many residents were actually excited by the thought of an eruption—but after the eruption of May 18, they no longer thought an erupting volcano was exciting. They thought it was very, very dangerous. (A lawsuit against the USGS for not properly informing people of the danger of the volcano is highlighted in the "Lawsuit!" sidebar on the following page.)

The Red Zone around the mountain turned out to be too small to save lives. Because geologists thought that the mountain would erupt *up,* and not *out,* they had not considered the effects of a horizontal blast. Despite reports that people died because they were in the Red Zone, in fact, all of the fatalities were in areas that were thought to be "safe."

Even after being warned, most people in the area did not see the volcano as dangerous. As one area resident put it, "I just thought some little puffs of smoke would come out and the lava would dribble down." The reality was much different.

The small town of Toutle (population 1,500) lies 25 miles (40 km) northwest of Mount St. Helens, just north of the point where the North and South Forks of the Toutle River join. Even though they were fairly close to the erupting mountain, few residents of the town reported hearing any sound when the volcano blew. Residents who happened to be outside did see the large mushroom cloud of ash emerging from the mountain's peak. Within minutes, they noticed that the air was becoming very warm. Trees and car windshields cracked from the heat. About 90 minutes after the eruption, the first bits of ash floated over the town, leaving a light dusting on everything. Once the hot mud hit the river, its temperature rose to 80°F (27°C). Because they were warned in time, people in low-lying areas near the river evacuated safely. About 200 homes were destroyed as the mud overflowed the banks of the rivers.

Bruce Nelson and Sue Ruff had gone camping with a couple of friends. Getting up early, they could not see Mount St. Helens, 14 miles (22.5 km) to the south. As they stood near the campfire, they saw a puff of smoke above the trees. Within minutes, the entire sky was filled with ash, and the wind blew like a hurricane. Huge trees fell, shaking the ground. Covering their faces with their shirts, Nelson and Ruff picked their way through the hot trees and climbed the closest hill as they tried to escape. After 30 minutes, ice and rock started falling on them. They took cover under some tree

Lawsuit!

After the eruption, the same agencies that were criticized for needlessly keeping people out of a beloved recreation area were accused of deliberately withholding information about how dangerous the mountain really was so that timber companies could continue their logging operations. The USGS received particularly harsh criticism for not predicting the timing and extent of the blast.

A lawsuit filed against the USGS for damages resulting from the blast was dismissed in 1985. The court ruled that there was no evidence that the USGS knew when and how the volcano would explode. As evidence, attorneys for the government pointed out that the USGS lost one of its own employees, David Johnston, because it thought that his observation post 6 miles (9.6 km) away from the volcano was perfectly safe. Because knowledge of volcano behavior is still being collected, it will be many years—if ever—before earth scientists will be able to predict with accuracy when a volcano will erupt, how it will erupt, and how long it will continue to erupt.

trunks. Nelson said to Ruff, "If we get out of this alive, you're going to marry me." Ruff agreed. (They did eventually get married.)

Ninety minutes later, they made it back to their camp. Instead, Dan Balch and Brian Thomas hailed them. Balch had severely burned his hands, and a falling trunk had shattered Thomas's hip. Nelson and Ruff tried to help them out of the area, but they were too badly injured. "My God! Don't leave me here to die!" Thomas gasped.

Assuring him that they would send help, Nelson and Ruff continued to struggle out of the forest. In the late afternoon they met another survivor, Grant Christensen. Nelson, Ruff, and Christensen walked until dusk. They were about to stop for the night when they heard a helicopter overhead. They shouted and stirred up the dust so that the crew could see them. The helicopter was able to land and move them to safety. Other helicopters picked up Thomas and Balch. They were lucky—but Nelson and Ruff's friends were not. The falling trees had crushed them.

In 2004—A Different Response

When Mount St. Helens started shaking again in late September 2004, emergency management teams from the state of Washington and the counties immediately surrounding the volcano got in touch with USGS and Pacific Northwest Seismographic Network scientists. There would be no delays in taking necessary action to keep people safe this time. Counties that could be affected by ash falls encouraged residents to assemble emergency kits with water, food, and portable radios that would allow them to stay at home for at least three days.

The Cascade Volcano Observatory issued warnings as the mountain moved to a more eruptive situation and evacuated people from areas deemed to be dangerous. Although curious watchers crowded the roadways and staked out good viewing locations, people remained a safe distance away. No one wished to see a repeat of the deaths from the 1980 eruption.

CHAPTER 4

Cleaning Up, Moving On

The eruption left a mess to clean up: ash in eastern Washington and mud in western Washington. The ash fall was not huge, but it was enough to disrupt life for a number of days. Airports and highways closed, and electricity was in short supply because damp ash caused electrical lines to short-circuit. So many people were calling friends that the telephone system became overloaded and was virtually closed down. Ash filled the sewage treatment system in Yakima, and raw sewage flowed into the Yakima River.

Furthermore, media coverage of the eruption had led people to cancel trips to Washington. Many people decided to vacation elsewhere, and some groups canceled conventions, meetings, and social gatherings—even those that were scheduled in parts of Washington (and even Oregon) that were not affected by the eruption.

A town in eastern Washington is covered with ash after the May 18 eruption of Mount St. Helens. (Photo courtesy of Douglas Kirkland/CORBIS)

Mount St. Helens dealt a double blow to Washington and Oregon—states that depended on tourism to boost the local economy. The eruption made a mess that had to be cleaned up, and it scared people away. Once the eruption quieted down, however, media coverage focused on the rare opportunity to see nature's reaction to a large volcanic event. Then Mount St. Helens became a tourist attraction in its own right—bringing in people from all over the world who wanted to see the mountain that had blown its top off.

Ash and Agriculture

The ash that drifted over eastern Washington and contributed to $100 million in crop losses (7 percent of normal value) during 1980 is the same ash that makes the area's soil rich and fertile. The ash had two primary effects. First, because it was lighter-colored than the soil on which it fell, the ash increased the *albedo* (the amount of sun reflected back from Earth). Because more sunlight was reflected than normal, the temperature of the soil dropped by as much as 18°F (10°C). Therefore, plants acted as if winter was coming and became *dormant* (inactive). By tilling the ground to bury the ash and leave soil from below on top of it, farmers were able to solve that problem.

Second, the ash was just the right size to plug up the holes that allow water to move through soil. So rain ran off the top of the ash instead of soaking into the ground. In other locations, the water pooled on the surface of the ash, and the ash then became as hard as concrete. On the other hand, the ash also kept soil moisture from evaporating. Although heavy rainfalls after the eruption did result in some local flooding due to runoff, for the most part the ash did not create serious, long-term problems for farmers.

The ash did create a temporary problem for the agriculture industry. The losses experienced by farmers after the Mount St.

Helens eruption depended upon what they were growing and where. Farmers, realizing they had a problem with all the ash falling on their crops, livestock, and equipment, became "experts on coping" to minimize damage, noted James Lyons, a researcher from Clark University in Massachusetts. Agriculture returned to normal within a year of the blast and remains an important source of income and employment in the state. The ash became a permanent part of the soil in eastern Washington.

Orchard Fruits

The Yakima Valley, just east of the Cascade Range, is famous for its orchards—apples, peaches, and apricots grow there in abundance. The apple crop emerged with little damage, because blossoms had been pollinated before the eruption. Growers just needed to get the ash off the leaves so that they had enough exposure to the Sun to allow photosynthesis—the process whereby plants create the sugars that they need to stay alive and produce fruit. Ash on leaves prevents photosynthesis and causes the leaves to burn when heated by the Sun. To remove the ash, farmers hired helicopters to blow the ash off the leaves. They also used ground-based blowers and wind machines normally used to protect their fruit from frost. When just a small amount of ash was left, they used water to wash it off. A 25 percent greater-than-average rainfall starting in the autumn of 1980 helped.

Peach and apricot growers were not so lucky. These fuzzy-skinned fruits were already forming when the clouds of ash fell on them. Because the fuzz held the ash, farmers were not able to remove it. The entire crop was lost.

Grasses

For farmers growing grasses—wheat and alfalfa—further to the east in the flat, arid region of Washington, the ash fall was both good and bad. For the wheat farmers, the ash that covered their fields turned out to be a bonanza of good fortune. The wheat had not yet "headed out"—that is, the "ear," or part of the wheat that is harvested and ground to make flour, had not formed. The ash just fell around the short, stiff shoots and helped to retain moisture in the soil. Because a lack of rain is always a problem for these wheat farmers, the ash, by holding in the soil's moisture, contributed to a bumper wheat crop for the year.

Not so lucky were the alfalfa farmers. Alfalfa is a grass grown to feed a variety of livestock. The alfalfa was just about ready for harvest when the ash fell and bent its slender leaves of grass over to the ground. The bent leaves held on to the ash. Most of the crop could not be harvested, and the alfalfa that farmers could harvest was full of dust. The total loss was $35 million. However, alfalfa is a perennial plant—the same plant grows back for several years. Farmers who had replanted their alfalfa fields within the preceding year just waited for the plants to come up again in 1981. The farmers who had not replanted in a number of years tilled their ash-covered plants back into the soil and planted new ones.

Berries

Berries are a significant crop in southwestern Washington and northwestern Oregon. Although they were not affected by the May 18 eruption, when the wind blew the ash east, Mount St. Helens's later eruptions occurred when the wind was blowing toward the west—right over the berry crops. The eruption of May 25 spread ash over western Washington's blueberry crop just before it was ready for harvesting. The damaged fruit could not be sold. Likewise, the June 12 eruption sent ash over southwestern Washington and northwestern Oregon, where it landed on the raspberry and strawberry crops. Approximately 75 percent of Oregon's raspberry crop was lost when the ash clung to the fuzzy berries. Forty percent of Washington's and Oregon's strawberry crops were lost when the ash pushed down the stems and leaves of the plants. This forced the strawberries down into the soil, where they rotted.

Insects

Although many insects are harmful to agriculture, insects like honeybees, wasps, yellow jackets, and bumblebees are needed to pollinate the flowers on fruit and vegetable plants. These insects were badly affected by the eruption. The ash wore away the waxy outer coverings of their bodies. These coverings helped them to retain moisture. The bee colonies in the Columbia Basin were particularly hard hit—12,000 of 15,000 bee colonies were either destroyed or badly damaged for a loss of $1 million.

Harmful insects also died. In particular, the grasshoppers died in such large numbers that farmers did not have to spray their fields to get rid of them in the summer following the eruption.

Timber—Down, but Not Out

The timber companies had been upset when the state put the blockades up on the roads, but then they realized that they had their own roads. They were going to continue their logging operations—potential eruption or not.

Although the Red Zone had been conveniently drawn so that Weyerhaeuser property was outside of it, some loggers were worried about the volcano. To calm their fears, Weyerhaeuser equipped them with devices that were supposed to measure how much ash was in the air. Weyerhaeuser officials said that they would provide timber workers with at least two hours' notice of dangerous conditions, allowing them enough time to evacuate. But Joel Hembree, safety representative for the loggers' union, bluntly said to crews, "All I can tell you guys is if it blows, it blows. Who's to say it won't happen tomorrow, or ten years down the line?"

Over 1,000 Weyerhaeuser employees continued to work in the forests around Mount St. Helens. Only because the eruption occurred on a Sunday morning—when loggers were not working— were there many fewer deaths than there might have been. Had the loggers been in their usual locations, hundreds would have died.

Three billion board feet of timber covering 150 square miles (390 km²) came down in the eruption. One board foot is a piece of wood 1 foot square (0.09 m²) and 1 inch (2.5 cm) thick. Much of it was on land owned by Weyerhaeuser and other timber companies. The immediate question was what should be done with the downed trees. Foresters determined that the trees had to be removed within four years. Otherwise, they would become unusable due to wood rot or beetles.

The private timber companies moved quickly to get the trees out of the area. Within a few weeks, more than 300 logging trucks per day were moving out of the Green River and North

These trees, about 14 miles (22 m) from the volcano, were felled by the force of the explosion or stripped of their branches by the extremely hot wind that followed the eruption on May 18. (Photo courtesy of Associated Press)

Fork–Toutle River area. When fully loaded, each truck carried 80 tons (73 mt) of trees. By the end of 1980, 600 trucks per day were hauling out logs that were mostly heading for sawmills in Japan. By the time the lumber companies were finished salvaging the timber, they had removed enough to build 85,000 homes. Despite the salvage operation, $400 million worth of timber was lost.

The removal of trees became a controversial issue. For the timber companies, every tree left lying on the ground was a loss of their investment, so every salvageable tree needed to come off the mountain. James Sedell of the USFS's Pacific Northwest Forest and Range Experiment Station was one of many biologists who wanted the trees left on the ground. "As a biologist," he said, "I'd like to leave it there because it's providing really diverse habitat and deflecting stream flow." Sedell and his colleagues worked to keep at least some of the trees on the ground so that water from rain and snowmelt would not run in sheets down the mountainside.

Scientists were able to keep the downed trees on the ground within the new "outdoor laboratory" of Mount St. Helens National Volcanic Monument, created in 1982. (The formation of the monument is further discussed in the "Creating a Monument" sidebar on the following page.) Weyerhaeuser and other timber firms, however, viewed their lands as a different sort of outdoor laboratory—in which they could determine how best to salvage their investment. First, they removed all the downed trees—even ones that could not be milled for lumber. If they left the dead trees on the ground, insects would move in to eat them and then eventually migrate to the new trees the firms planned to plant.

While the tree removal continued, scientists were working to figure out the best way to plant seedlings on the ash-covered hillsides. Weyerhaeuser had never reforested an area covered with deep ash. The company could not afford to plant millions of seedlings and then watch them die. By digging down through the ash until they reached good soil and then planting the seedlings, they were able to create a new forest.

Planting was a massive job. Weyerhaeuser employees planted between 300 and 600 seedlings per acre (0.4 ha) between January and June of 1981. Due to careful preparation of the ground and wise selection of tree species, survival rates were extremely high. In elevations below 2,800 feet (853 m), the company planted Douglas firs, of which over 90 percent survived, and red alders, of which over 95 percent survived. Above 2,800 feet they planted noble firs, of which over 80 percent survived. The trees will be ready to harvest when they are about 60 years old.

Twenty years after the eruption, only half the amount of logging was being done compared with before the eruption. But the eruption itself was responsible for less than half of that decline. Washington's economy was in bad shape for most of those years and was responsible for most of the reduction in logging. (The tourism industry has since become a small, but increasingly important, source of income in the Mount St. Helens area, as told in the "A Change for the Better?" sidebar on the following page.)

Creating a Monument

In 1982 Congress passed legislation creating the Mount St. Helens National Volcanic Monument. The monument preserves 109,900 acres (44,500 ha) of land, a compromise between environmentalists, who wanted more land preserved, and the timber companies, who wanted much less preserved. Within the monument, no attempts were made to alter what the volcano had left. Blown-down trees were not harvested, and plants were not brought in. The monument was created to be a natural laboratory for scientific study and for the public to observe the effects of the volcano for themselves.

Ash and Mudflow Damage

Although the ash falling over eastern Washington was an inconvenience and made a substantial mess that had to be cleaned up, it did not damage many structures. Realizing that the weight of the ash on building roofs might cause them to collapse, people scooped it off with shovels. Yet the ash was considerably heavier than the dry snow that typically falls in eastern Washington, and unlike snow, it would never melt. Yakima police chief Jack LaRue remembered, "It took a while to figure out how to clean up. The

A Change for the Better?

The Gifford Pinchot National Forest, where Mount St. Helens was located, had long been a favorite camping, hiking, and fishing spot. People would arrive with their out-door gear, purchase some groceries, and spend several days in the woods. Those who were not keen on camping would stay in local motels, returning in the evening after a day of hiking. But once Mount St. Helens erupted, most visitors did not come to stay—they came to look. Instead of motel rooms, they needed places to sit down and have meals.

Local businesses scrambled to meet the needs of these new tourists. Restaurants and casual food stands opened up to feed hungry visitors who wanted to see the eruption's devastation. About 500,000 people a year visit the Mount St. Helens National Volcanic Monument, and they have provided a much-needed boost to the economy. Yet tourism has not replaced the losses of the timber industry, and overall, tourism has not become a truly significant part of the economy in the surrounding area.

stuff didn't sweep and it didn't wash away. Water just turned it into a paste." Once the paste dried, it turned into a cement-like material. Cities and counties needed to scoop it up and haul it out of town.

Because of its abrasive nature and ability to clog up small openings, the ash created many problems for motor vehicles of all types (cars, trucks, farm equipment) and aircraft. The ash clogged the air filters on cars because the air was being sucked in from near the ground, where the ash was. About 5,000 people were stranded on roads in eastern Washington on the day of the eruption. There were 2,000 stranded in the town of Ritzville, 195 miles (315 km) away from the crater. With a population of just 1,900 people, town residents worked to house all of their unexpected guests. Churches, schools, and private homes took in people. According to motel operator Diane Keetch, "We had people staying in the basement. Total strangers volunteered to share rooms."

Within two days of the eruption, half of all state police, local police, and emergency vehicles were no longer running. In addition to the clogged air filters, the sharp edges of the ash particles damaged the automatic transmissions, preventing the vehicles from changing gears. Aircraft were grounded until runways could be cleared of ash so it would not be sucked into their engines and damage them. (The medical effects of breathing the ash are discussed in the "Masking against the Ash" sidebar on the following page.)

More damaging than the ash were the massive mudflows that surged down the Toutle and Cowlitz rivers and eventually into the Columbia River. The mudflow that began on the afternoon of the eruption dumped 3.9 million cubic yards (3 million m³) of sediment into the Columbia. The sediment reduced the depth of its shipping channel (the part of the river used by oceangoing ships) from 39 feet (11.9 m) to 13 feet (4 m) for a length of 4 miles (6.4 km). Some ships were trapped at the Port of Portland, while others could not get to the port from the Pacific Ocean. The channel was partially cleared by May 23, but it was not completely cleared until November. In all, Portland lost $5 million in shipping revenue. Other costs resulting from the Mount St. Helens disaster are highlighted in the "Costs of the Eruption" sidebar on page 52.

The Flood Hazard

Unlike some other natural disasters, such as hurricanes, tornadoes, and floods, that usually have a starting point and an ending point, a volcano is a disaster that can keep on causing problems even after the ash stops falling and the vents stop steaming. One of those continuing hazards is from mudflows.

In the case of Mount St. Helens, the eruption had left thousands of tons of loose material on the mountain. A heavy rain would send water cascading over the ash, which did not allow it to sink in. Instead, the rain would pick up some of the ash on its way down the mountain. Within a matter of hours, rivers of

Masking against the Ash

When the ash started falling out of the sky, residents were concerned about the long-term effects of getting the ash particles into their lungs. Over 3,300 students at Washington State University at Pullman dropped out of school before the spring term ended because they were afraid of lung problems caused by the ash. Until the danger could be determined, people were told to stay indoors. If they had to go outside, they were advised to put on special masks usually worn to filter out dust and pollen. The masks would reduce the amount of ash that they inhaled. However, there were not enough masks for everyone. President Jimmy Carter promised to immediately send 2 million masks. The Minnesota Mining and Manufacturing Company (3M) sent every mask it had—almost 1 million—to Washington state.

Within a few days, medical authorities determined that residents would need to inhale large quantities of ash over many years to suffer any adverse effects. Only 2 percent of the mineral silica in the ash was the kind that could lead to *silicosis* (a condition that makes it difficult for people to breathe). Of course, local residents were not facing the same conditions as those people who were trapped on the mountain in the thickest part of the ash fall. That ash was so thick that it prevented people from breathing at all, so they suffocated.

Although ash drifted over a few neighboring towns and onto adjacent roadways during the 2004 eruption, no one was greatly inconvenienced. Some local residents did pull out their masks just in case, but there was no need to mask this time.

muddy water would be heading down the valleys away from the mountain. As Dick Janda, a scientist from the USGS, warned, "If I lived in Kelso or Longview, [Washington,] I'd keep my ear on the radio all the time." In other words, there would not be much time to get out of the way of the raging water.

In an attempt to prevent this potential danger to people living downstream from the mountain, the Army Corps of Engineers built two small dams to hold back the sediment-filled water. Both failed within eight months after the blast. Much more sediment built up behind the dams than the engineers had expected. Clearly, other measures needed to be taken.

The possibility of flooding in downstream rivers—the Toutle, Cowlitz, and Columbia—increased with each load of sediment that settled on their riverbeds. There was less room for water as the bottoms of the riverbeds filled in. The Army Corps of Engineers hired 28 contractors who worked in shifts, 20 hours a day, six days a week, to remove the sediment. By late autumn of 1980, they were removing 12.4 million cubic feet (350,000 m³) of sediment and debris each day.

The engineers next tried sealing off the Toutle at the point where it flowed into the Cowlitz in order to keep the sediment out. The Cowlitz could carry very little water, so even a moderate rainstorm would be enough to flood out the 45,000 people who lived along its banks.

The U.S. Army Corps of Engineers began a dredging program on the Toutle River, shown here, as well as the Cowlitz and Columbia rivers, in order to remove sediment from the 1980 eruption and any additional sedimentation that occurred afterward. (Photo courtesy of U.S. Geological Survey)

The Costs of the Eruption

The first two major eruptions caused $1.8 billion in property and crop damage due to mudflows and ash falls. That included $75 million to move the ash off the roads and $85 million to repair or replace 27 bridges and 169 miles (272 km) of roads. The short-term economic losses—lost business, cleanup costs—totaled $860 million.

But there was a greater price than just the financial cost of the Mount St. Helens eruption. Even though the ash in the air did not turn out to be a health hazard for the people in the shadow of the volcano, the psychological effects of living through the eruption and seeing their property buried under mounds of ash and mud continued for years. People who lived along the routes to the mountain experienced symptoms of depression for many years after the eruption. They had trouble sleeping, were often irritable, and felt powerless in the face of the overwhelming force of the mountain. Some people who had been rescued from the mountain when their companions and family members had died also had to cope with feelings of guilt on top of their grief.

The rainstorm that everyone had been dreading occurred on Christmas Day 1980: Warm rains that added to the snow already on the ground produced an equivalent of 8 inches (20.3 cm) of rain coming down the side of Mount St. Helens. The runoff broke through the dam on the North Fork of the Toutle and, with its load of sediment and debris, caused extensive damage to the Interstate-5 bridge over the Toutle.

CHAPTER 5

Life Emerges from the Ashes

After flying over the devastated area just days after the eruption, former President Jimmy Carter remarked, "There is no way to prepare oneself for the sight we beheld this morning. It's the worst thing I've ever seen." The effect on plants and animals was immediate and dramatic, particularly within the Blast Zone. Despite the landscape's appearance, however, not all living things were killed. Pockets of life remained: under soil protected by snow and ice, behind sheltered ridges, and deep within trees, insects and small mammals rode out the eruption to repopulate the area surrounding Mount St. Helens.

Ten days after the big eruption, Mount St. Helens is covered in mud deposited by an avalanche that followed the blast. A helicopter carrying scientists ready to continue research lands in the mud. (Photo courtesy of Roger Ressmeyer/CORBIS)

Old-growth forests (trees that had not been planted by people) of Pacific silver fir and mountain hemlock had surrounded Mount St. Helens. Those trees close to the mountain were scorched, blown down, and in some cases, completely ripped out of the ground. Yet those that were protected by layers of snow and ice so that their root systems remained intact kept a spark of life. Plants outside the Blast Zone were not killed outright. If they caught the heaviest part of the ash fall, they were usually unable to recover and died within a few days.

Lakes, Streams, and Rivers

The mountain lakes in the path of destruction, such as Spirit Lake, were instantaneously changed from being clear, blue, and full of fish and *amphibians* to being black and full of downed trees. They also emitted an extremely foul odor. The fish in Spirit Lake were killed by the pyroclastic flow.

Spirit Lake can be seen here following the 1980 eruption. (Photo courtesy of U.S. Geological Survey)

The resulting debris dam (a barrier made up of tightly packed logs, rocks, and mud) held in the putrid, debris-filled water. After the blast, 33 times more ash, soil, and organic material floated in the lake than before. Because sunlight could not penetrate the water, the algae died. Bacteria, including those that cause pneumonia and Legionnaires' disease, became the dominant forms of life. Visiting a few weeks after the eruption, researcher James Sedell had planned to use a raft to paddle onto Spirit Lake and collect water samples. Unfortunately, his boat sprang a leak, so he decided to wade into the water. That was a big mistake. Sedell recalled his experience in the dark, bubbling water: "We're talking of water that had several million bacteria cells per cubic centimeter. I was sicker than a dog about 48 hours later."

Four months after the eruption, the bacteria had used up all the oxygen. The ash in the water was laden with sulfur, and this produced its typical "rotten egg" smell. Although Spirit Lake was the most well known of the affected lakes, 169 lakes suffered similarly from the blast.

Mudflows radically changed streams and rivers. Carrying a large load of rocks and logs, fast-moving mud ripped up the sides of the many small streams that drained the mountainside, leaving large rocks behind in the middle of the streambed. The "Forever Dredging" sidebar on the following page tells about the removal of sediment from the rivers.

Animals—Smooth, Furry, and Feathered

Despite the problems in the lakes and streams, amphibians (tailed frogs, Pacific giant salamanders, and newts) survived in large numbers because they were hibernating in the mud at the bottom of the water. Pacific tree frogs also emerged relatively unscathed.

Mammals whose homes were the forest trees and shrubs within the Blast Zone were killed instantly and in large numbers.

Forever Dredging

The Columbia River must be *dredged* (the sediment must be removed from the river bottom) regularly so that ships can sail up the river to Portland. After the eruption, the sediment produced by the volcano continued to move downstream. Over 6 feet (1.8 m) of sand and gravel were dumped by the Cowlitz River into the mouth of the Columbia River at Astoria, Oregon. The river had just been dredged when Mount St. Helens exploded. Engineers needed to dredge out the quickly deposited sediment to get river traffic moving again. All of the loose material left on the side of the mountain will continue to wash into the river and require additional dredging. The sediment problem in the rivers will not disappear quickly.

Mount St. Helens had been home to over 6,000 black-tail deer and over 5,000 Roosevelt elk before the eruption. Only a handful of them living on the edge of the Blast Zone had survived. Over 1,000 coyotes died, along with several hundred bobcats and black bears. Only a few mountain lions and mountain goats had lived in the vicinity of the volcano before its eruption and none were found afterward.

Beavers also died in large numbers as mudflows swept their dams downstream. Smaller mammals that spent most of their time above ground, like hares, gray squirrels, and golden-mantled ground squirrels, also died by the tens of thousands. Those animals that lived under the snow- and ice-covered ground, however, survived in large numbers. Pocket gophers and moles that lived in an extensive system of underground tunnels snaking beneath the dense forest emerged to find a completely new landscape compared to the one they had left behind in the late autumn. With their stash of roots below ground, they had been able to survive. While the heat and ash adversely affected the animals on the surface, the insulating qualities of the snow and ice had prevented the *subterranean* animals from becoming too warm.

Most members of at least 12 other mammal species (including several types of mice and gophers), in addition to the pocket gophers and moles, survived the blast. Deer mice, Pacific jumping mice, wandering shrews, voles, weasels, mink, and muskrat had all been sufficiently protected by snow and ice to survive. The Pacific jumping mice are hibernators and slept through the entire eruption, only to emerge several weeks later, when they started waking up for the summer.

Birds in the Blast Zone were killed immediately. Thousands of the birds that had died—especially the hermit thrushes and gray jays—lived year-round in the area, so there was no way that wildlife biologists could get an accurate count. The State Department of Game did estimate that about 27,000 grouse (a chicken-sized ground bird) were killed. The Mount St. Helens area was not home to any birds that were in danger of extinction, so their deaths did not eliminate entire species.

On the western side of the mountain, the hot mudflows that overflowed the North Fork–Toutle and Cowlitz rivers killed all the adult salmon there within just a few hours, as the abrasive edges of the ash cut through their gills. Including the small "fingerlings" being raised in hatcheries, officials estimated that 11 million fish of all kinds died because of the eruption. The ash also filled and destroyed the spawning grounds where salmon return to reproduce. Due to water temperatures of at least 85°F (30°C), most living things died in the smaller streams that fed into the rivers. A very small number of fish such as brook trout, rainbow trout, and cutthroats, and bottom-dwelling invertebrates such as crayfish, were able to survive because the debris formed small pools where they were able to hide.

Tiny Creatures

Millions of insects were killed in the blast—but the hardy wood beetles that had made their homes in the centers of large trees popped back out once the scorched trees had cooled down. In addition to the beetles, insects, spiders, and invertebrate species that lived below the ground and within logs also survived. Researchers in the area saw ants, spiders, millipedes, and centipedes within a few days of the blast. (Entomologist Rick Sugg of the University of Washington found only two of the twelve species of ants that had lived near the mountain before the eruption.) The beetles had the best chance of long-term survival, since they had sturdy bodies and an abundance of downed trees to provide food.

Insects that were dependent upon the tender shoots of green plants for their food flew into the area shortly after the eruption and died quickly. These soft bodied flying insects died when the ash wore away the protective covering that helped them retain moisture. Tiny ash particles also plugged the holes through which they breathed, causing them to suffocate.

Even insects hundreds of miles away from the blast were killed when ash started to fall. Insects that were a major food for fish were killed in large numbers in northern Idaho when they were smothered by ash that fell to the bottom of streams and lakes. These insects included the *larval* (immature) forms of flies, gnats, and midges. Once the ash settled, however, these insects returned to the streams within a few weeks. The return of plants and animals to the area around the mountain is discussed further in the "Coming Back from a Beating" sidebar below.

Coming Back from a Beating

Clearly, many of the plants and animals that lived in the paths of the ash falls, mudflows, avalanches, and pyroclastic flows of the volcano were wiped out in the first few hours after the eruption. But enough lived to start the recovery process. Even a dead tree provides a spot for a bird to perch or perhaps make a home. The shelter of that tree may be just enough to give seeds in the bird's droppings a chance to take root. Once one plant starts to grow, other life joins it. As University of Washington botanist Roger del Moral stated, "While it took a beating, life was never obliterated from Mount St. Helens."

CHAPTER 6

Nature's Recovery

Even though the area surrounding Mount St. Helens, covered with gray rock and ash, looked much like the Moon's surface, life returned very quickly. But it was not the life that had been there before the eruption—it was very simple life. These simple life forms would be critical to the more advanced life forms that would follow.

Within two weeks of the eruption, the edges of the North Fork of the Toutle River were already home to large colonies of filamentous bacteria (dominated by those bacterial species found in sewage plants) and cyanobacteria, also known as blue-green algae because of their color. Both were apparently able to survive because they were feeding on the organic chemicals that were

Spirit Lake, at the base of Mount St. Helens, recovered in stages over a 20-year period. (Photo courtesy of U.S. Geological Survey)

leaching out of the downed trees that crisscrossed the area (the chemicals were dissolving when the water moved through the trees and then flowing out of the trees along with the water).

Spirit Lake's Revival

The rapidly exploding bacteria population in Spirit Lake used up all the available oxygen in the water within a few days after the eruption. So while the lake looked dead and *smelled* dead, in fact, it was teeming with millions of one-celled organisms called *methanogens* that mostly live in swamps where all the oxygen has been consumed. (Methanogens also are active in disposing of waste at sewage treatment plants.) Scientists analyzing these primitive bacteria found that they were feeding on sulfur and metals in the water. The ability to consume these materials made them very similar to the kinds of life forms that lived billions of years ago. Mosquitoes that rode in on the wind soon joined the bacteria. In order to thrive, mosquitoes need better water than Spirit Lake had to offer and more animals to bite for their food. Nevertheless, these newly arrived mosquitoes did make fine meals for the returning birds.

As the ash, soil, and other debris floating in the water gradually sank down to the bottom, more sunlight was able to penetrate the lake's surface, and algae returned. As the algae increased, they slowly changed the chemistry of the water. The oxygen level increased, and it once again became home to a variety of plants and animals. As fall and then winter came to Mount St. Helens, rain and snow provided fresh water, and colder temperatures slowed down the rapidly reproducing bacteria. By 1986, Spirit Lake was as clear as it had been before the eruption. Blown-down logs still cover more than half its surface.

Ten years after the eruption, there were still no fish in the lake. By the 20th anniversary of the eruption, trout had appeared, but no one knows how they got there. Someone may have placed them there, or eggs may have survived in the muddy bottom.

Plants

At first glance, it appeared that plants had been wiped away from a large area surrounding the volcano. Although the top of each plant may have died, the entire plant was not gone. Especially when protected by snow and ice, the roots survived and started sending out new shoots within a few weeks.

One researcher looking for these plants was plant ecologist Jerry Franklin. Riding in a helicopter to Ryan Lake, about 12 miles (19.3 km) from the crater, just two and a half weeks after the eruption, Franklin hopped out to look around. "We didn't know what to expect," he recalled. "We stepped across a ditch on the edge of the road and right away we saw fireweed coming up through the ash." Other plants were not far away. In areas of higher snowpack that had not taken a direct hit from pyroclastic flows, smaller shrubs and trees had been sufficiently protected and emerged more or less unharmed. Even more plants appeared in the Blow-down and Scorch zones. Thistle, pearly everlasting, and blackberries—in addition to the fireweed—pushed up through more than a foot of ash.

Scientists were amazed at how quickly plant life recovered from the eruption, although it will be at least 100 years before the landscape of Mount St. Helens resembles the lush, heavily wooded environment it was before the May 18 eruption. (Photo courtesy of BARRY SWEET/Landov)

Plant life was greatly aided by the efforts of the small but mighty pocket gophers—sometimes dubbed the heroes of the recovery. As these creatures moved about, they would dig up to the surface, pushing soil in front of them and mixing the ash into the ground below. The little gophers also moved around a special fungus—*mycorrhizal fungus*—that helps to provide plants with the nitrogen that they need to grow. The mounds of fertile soil that the gophers left behind became oases for incoming seeds of lupine, fireweed, and thimbleberry, giving them a chance to take root, sprout, and grow.

Areas around the crater's steam vents also became hospitable areas for plants. As the steam cooled and the moisture condensed out of the air, it provided enough water to allow windblown fern and moss spores to start growing.

Within two months of the blast, USFS biologists Jim MacMahon and Charlie Crisafulli were actively looking for any kind of plant life within the "pumice plains"—the area directly in front of the crater where over 300 feet (91 m) of pumice had landed. Scientists had assumed that of all the areas surrounding Mount St. Helens, this would be the only one where absolutely nothing would survive the blast. Any plants that appeared would need to be good "colonizers." As Crisafulli explained, "Some plants have good dispersive qualities, but can't survive once they get here. Other species would do beautifully in this environment but have no way to get here." That means that a good colonizer plant has seeds that fly on the wind and that can take root and live in poor environments.

After several days of flying back and forth in a helicopter, Crisafulli and MacMahon spotted a flash of green. Upon landing, they found a single lupine. The biologists staked out a 2,420-square-foot (225-m²) plot, roping it off to make sure that no one trampled the plant or its surroundings.

The lupine was able to thrive in the pumice—which had very few nutrients—because lupines are "nitrogen fixers." Unlike most other plants, they are able to pull the essential nutrient nitrogen from the air when it does not exist in the soil. (The air is almost 80 percent nitrogen.) By the time that winter set in, this single lupine plant was 2 feet (0.6 m) in diameter. By the next summer, the nutrients that the lupine had added to the pumice allowed other windblown plant seeds to sprout and grow. False dandelions and pearly everlasting, plus the frequently appearing fireweed, started growing in the plot. As they floated by, seeds and insects alighted on these plants. Many of the insects stayed, and when they eventually died, their rotting bodies added more nutrients to the soil. (Another source of nutrients for the plants is highlighted in the "From Death Comes Life" sidebar on this page.) More plant seeds sprouted. By the end of the third summer after the blast, researchers counted a total of 24,000 individual plants where the one solitary lupine had started to grow in the summer of 1980. After 10 years, the plot held 164,000 plants.

From Death Comes Life

Almost all the elk near Mount St. Helens were killed by the eruption. Their bodies lay scattered throughout the devastated area. As the bodies decayed, they provided nutrients to the ash beneath them. A year after the blast, patches of green about the size of small blankets could be seen from the air about 7 miles (11.3 km) from the volcano. Upon closer inspection, researchers found an elk's skeleton within each patch. As seeds had become trapped within it, the remains had provided food for the growing plants.

Three years after the eruption, biologists had found specimens of 90 percent of the 230 plant species that had lived in the area before it had been devastated. Within 10 years, visitors to the Blast Zone were able to see small patches of green—sturdy colonies of plants—against the gray pumice.

According to botanist A.B. Adams, areas that had been covered by deep mudflows did not provide good homes to most plants. The hard surface of the ash and rock did not allow seeds to take root. In general, the very ends of mudflows tended to offer better opportunities for plants to take root. These were areas where most of the soil, roots, and organic material picked up by the flowing mud were deposited. Once again most plants sprouted from seeds that had flown in on the wind.

Although areas that were hit with large amounts of ash had a hard time supporting plant life, those areas with a moderate amount of ash benefited from it. For the first two or three years after the eruption, this ash helped to retain moisture in the ground. Weyerhaeuser, while replanting trees on its land, also observed that the ash reduced the number of weeds that grew around the newly planted trees. Some ash had to be pushed away when the trees were planted, to make sure the root systems were in good soil—the ash was not very fertile. According to Ross Gilchrist of Weyerhaeuser, "The vegetation that did come back was very, very healthy and for the most part bigger, taller than the usual average height for the vegetation in that area."

Biologists who are studying the recovery think that by the time 100 years have passed (if there are no more big eruptions before then), a visitor to the area will have a difficult time finding the effects of the 1980 eruption. Botanist Robert H. Mohlenbrock of Southern Illinois University wrote, "Scientists studying the mountain should still be observing the effects of the great 1980 eruption well into the next millennium." The flattened top of Mount St. Helens will remain, of course, as a reminder.

Insects and Spiders

Insects had been arriving via the wind since the mountain stopped erupting—almost 1,500 different species in the first few months. Flies and wasps were the first insects to arrive from the air, but there was nothing for them to eat, and most of them just became food for birds. Spiders—75 different species—also arrived on the wind and settled near the crater. The area was a tough place to survive. Grasshoppers arrived and died in large numbers, since there were few plants to eat. Beetles were happy to feast on their bodies. When the insects and spiders died, nitrogen and phosphorous from their decaying bodies returned to the soil and provided important nutrients for future plants.

Amphibians

Many amphibians and the eggs they had laid had survived the initial blast. Once they emerged from hibernation, these animals found a world that was almost totally without predators. One year later, thousands of Western toads were hopping all over parts of the mountain. The loss of trees was also an advantage for the toads. When the area was heavily forested, the shade had reduced the amount of algae that could grow in lakes. With the trees gone and more sunlight streaming in, the amount of algae increased, and the tadpoles (infant toads) had plenty to eat.

In other protected pockets were thousands of rough-skinned newts, Pacific tree frogs, and brown salamanders. Of the 15 different species of salamander that had lived near Mount St. Helens before the blast, 12 species recovered and established colonies in the 120 new lakes and ponds. With their predators gone, all of the amphibians experienced an increase in population, because a higher-than-normal number of their young survived.

Fish

Millions of fish had died when the hot mudflows filled the rivers. The big concern was Chinook salmon. Salmon provide over $160 million a year to Washington's economy. If the rivers, holding 10 to 100 times more sediment than before the blast, were not clear enough when the salmon swam upstream to lay their eggs in the spring of 1981, there would be few young salmon the next year. A year after the blast, however, adult salmon returned in great numbers, and biologists labeled the spring spawning run as excellent. The scientists collected thousands of eggs and sent them to fish hatcheries to ensure a good supply of little fish.

Despite the success of the salmon, it took a number of years for the streams and rivers to heal completely. After 10 years, the South Fork of the Toutle River was once again filled with steelhead trout.

Yet the river had some help. State fisheries biologists closed the river to fishing after the eruption to give returning fish a chance to reproduce.

Mammals

Within a few days of the eruption, deer and elk started to explore the Blast Zone. They did not stay—there was nothing to eat. But their hooves started to break up the ash, giving water a place to pool and providing a potential home for seeds. As forest ecologist Peter Frenzen put it, "They [elk] can really tear up the soil."

Three years after the eruption, almost all the mammals were back, although in much smaller numbers than before. Twenty years after the eruption, in 2000, the mammals were back at full strength. The elk herd numbered 3,000 due to an abundance of grasses that had returned to the area. But the elk were not helpful to young trees. Elk especially liked to scrape the *velvet* (a soft covering) off their antlers by rubbing them against the lodgepole pines that Weyerhaeuser had replanted. In doing so, they rubbed the bark off the young trees, and the trees died. As the pine trees got bigger and shaded the ground, the amount of grass decreased, and the elk herd did not grow as rapidly.

Beavers, totally wiped out by the blast, started to return within a few years. These animals need trees to make dams; as willows and cottonwoods started to take root, the beavers came to stay. Along the South Fork of the Toutle River, beavers have been actively harvesting trees and building dams. As one researcher put it, "It looks like a beaver farm out there." Beaver ponds also make good homes for trout and salmon, so their work will lead to greater populations of fish.

In addition to the elk, snowshoe hares and coyotes also returned to the area in large numbers. Only a small herd of mountain goats had lived at Mount St. Helens before the eruption, and just a few have been seen in the last few years.

CHAPTER 7

Scientific Discovery

The new "natural laboratory" that was Mount St. Helens became the site of hundreds of scientific observations. (The close-up view that scientists had is highlighted in the "Braving the Volcano" sidebar on the following page.) Wildlife experts studied herds of Roosevelt elk. Entomologists (scientists who study insects) researched the effect of sediment and ash on stream insects—important food for fish. Other scientists studied the breeding habits of rough-skinned newts. Botanists studied how plants were able to make their way to the surface after being buried by ash. Ecologists, who look at all facets of life within an area, studied how environments recover from major changes that result from volcanic eruptions.

After the eruption, Mount St. Helens became a living laboratory for biologists, botanists, and ecologists. In this picture, a geologist studies erosion of the Toutle River. (Photo courtesy of Gary Braasch/CORBIS)

Biological Discoveries

One of the most exciting finds for scientists was the presence of microorganisms that were living under the rocks in the 208°F (98°C) heat of the steam vents surrounding the crater. They were very similar to *archaebacteria* (from the Greek word *archaio*, meaning "ancient"), animals that oceanographers have found living near hot deep-sea vents. These tiny animals exist under conditions that kill most other organisms.

Erosion—the washing away of surface materials by wind or water—is usually considered to be a disaster all its own. Strong winds can carry away valuable topsoil, leaving farmers with rock-strewn ground. Water from rain or snowmelt can pick up small bits of dirt and carry it down mountainsides. Although the surface of an entire hillside may leave with the water, a more likely occurrence is that the running water will form small channels that grow into large, ugly gullies. At first, at Mount St. Helens, the denuded mountainside covered with loose ash and small pumice was particularly at risk. The concern in the summer of 1980 was that the loose sediment would race down the hillside and into the streams and rivers. The sediment would fill up the riverbed and lead to flooding.

The Soil Conservation Service had an idea. This organization had been formed in the early 20th century to ensure that soil was not lost due to erosion. Using $20 million in federal funds, it would seed and fertilize the Blast Zone. But of the 13 species of grass that it planned to use, only the pine lupine was a species native to the area. Scientists who wanted the devastated area to recover without outside help did not greet this news with enthusiasm. If these non-native seeds were

Braving the Volcano

Researchers started studying the volcano up close just a few days after the eruption stopped. The only way in and out of the Blast Zone was by helicopter. Helicopter pilots kept their "choppers" going while the scientists (wearing gas masks) scrambled across the pumice plain, collecting samples. One scientist said it was like "walking on the moon." There was one big difference: The Moon is cold—the ground that the scientists were walking on was still hot. The temperature just a few inches below their feet was several hundred degrees.

planted, the scientists would never know how an area that had been virtually wiped clean of vegetation would come back to life.

The Soil Conservation Service did not abandon its plan, but it did reduce the area to be seeded from 200 square miles (518 km²) to 33 square miles (85 km²). Helicopters dropped the seed and fertilizer in September and October. Most of the fertilizer blew away in the wind, and the seeds, sitting on sterile ground, did not sprout. Instead, when the rains came they all washed down to the floor of the valley. As Jerry Franklin noted, "It was a waste of money, it didn't stop erosion, and it messed up a nice, clean study of *succession*." (Succession is the biological theory of the way that plants and animals repopulate an area.)

What happened next surprised scientists. The areas where running water formed gullies in the ash were the places most likely to see plants sprout, because the water cut down through the ash until soil was visible. Two things then happened. First, if there were still roots left in the soil, they sent up new shoots. Second, when new plant seeds blew in, they had both soil and moisture to give them a head start. As a result, the eroded areas are the ones with the most plant life. This discovery never would have been made if Soil Conservation Service scientists had replanted the entire area instead of watching to see how nature would take care of the problem. (Chance played a significant role in the recovery of the area, as described in the "Role of Chance" sidebar on the following page.)

Plant biologists had also thought that forests grew after a series of plants had come up in the same area first. Succession held that grasses would grow first. Shrubs would follow them, and then after several decades had passed, the tall trees of the forest would take over. But this did not happen after the Mount St. Helens eruption. The plants that appeared first were the plants whose seeds landed and took root first. Lupine, pearly everlasting, and fireweed sprang up instead of grasses, because they were better suited to the environment than native grasses were.

Biologists also were surprised to find that very small mammals sometimes travel 1 mile (1.6 km) or more in their search for new habitat. On Mount St. Helens, tiny shrews—weighing only 0.25 ounces (7 g), or about the same as a nickel—walked up to 2 miles (3.2 km) across rock and debris to set up their new homes.

The animal colonizers that survived and reproduced successfully were those that were "opportunists and generalists." Ecologist Charlie Crisafulli explains, "They can switch hit—they can eat seeds, insects, or green vegetation. They're prolific breeders and not tightly tied to any one habitat." Animals that could only survive on one kind of food did not live very long.

Using traps, entomologist John Edwards from the University of Washington calculated that in the summer of 1980, over 1,000 pounds (454 kg) of insects of landed in the Blast Zone. Since most of these (flies, gnats, and midges) had nothing to eat, they became food for other animals or died and became nutrients for the soil. On the other hand, the beetles, which ate almost anything, thrived. Larger mammals, like the elk, could wander in and out of the Blast Zone. They ate what they could find, leaving behind seeds of plants from outside the zone in their droppings, stirring up the soil with their hooves, and basically making the area more hospitable for other forms of life.

As Peter Frenzen pointed out, "There are relatively few players here, so it is easier to see the relationships [between plants and animals]. It is easier to figure things out." These easily observed interactions between colonizing plants and animals in the Mount St. Helens area held many surprises. Weyerhaeuser forester Dick Ford said, "Nature can take a lot more punishment than we give it credit for. Animals have a remarkable ability to adapt to changes in their environment."

The eruptive period that started in late September 2004 produced so little ash that the surrounding area's recovery was unaffected. Biological research continues in the early 21st century on

Mount St. Helens, but funding for long-term projects has decreased in the years since the 1980 eruption.

Geological Discoveries

Geologists had been puzzled for many years about the source of hummocky deposits (mounds of dirt and rock) that are present near some volcanoes. One place with such deposits was the Shasta River valley in northern California, near Mount Shasta. Geologists had been working since the 1930s to figure out where the strange mounds and hills that dotted the valley might have come from. Glacial and stream action had been proposed as two solutions. Others thought they were just very small volcanoes.

Once the geologists saw the remains of the collapse of Mount St. Helens's north flank, they had the solution. *Hummocks* resulted from huge landslides, and the mounds of the Shasta River valley came from a volcano that collapsed over 300,000 years ago. Acting on that insight, geologists have identified over 400 prehistoric debris avalanches. Such events had been considered rare, but now scientists think that they are fairly common.

After their close observation of the expanding lava dome within Mount St. Helens's crater, geologists also determined that they could actually predict the dome's behavior based on a number of measurements. These included data from seismographs that measure earth movement, the amount of dome swelling, the

The Role of Chance

After watching the progress of the recovery of plants and animals in the devastated area over a 20-year period, scientists discovered that it was largely based on chance. The plants that survived the blast did so because they were in the right place at the right time. In some cases, plants just a few yards away were killed. Many of the plants were saved because the eruption took place when there was still a lot of snow on the ground, covering them. Had the eruption occurred in August, the snow would have been gone and more plants would have been killed. Some small burrowing animals survived because the eruption occurred during the day, when most of them were asleep. Had Mount St. Helens erupted at night, many of these animals would have been on the surface instead of safely lodged in their underground homes.

Willie Scott, a scientist in charge of the U.S. Geological Survey Cascades Volcano Observatory in Vancouver, Washington, studies recordings from an earthquake that hit Seattle in February 2001. Scientists hope that lessons learned from the Mount St. Helens disaster can prevent loss of life and environmental damage in future disasters. (Photo courtesy of Associated Press)

number and size of cracks in the dome surface, and the presence of gases within the crater. By analyzing the collected data, scientists can identify potential changes in the dome that may provide clues about possible future eruptions.

Geologists also determined that one reason the gas pressure built up to such a high level within Mount St. Helens was that its magma contained a high percentage of silica. When magma is high in silica, it becomes very sticky and tends to plug up the vents that normally allow gases to escape. Geologists now monitor the amount of gas being emitted from Mount St. Helens and remain alert for decreases in emissions. A decrease might mean that the pressure is building up and an eruption might occur.

As a result of the eruption, scientists also discovered that the ash plumes from volcanoes can be accurately tracked by satellite. Ash clouds in the atmosphere can severely damage jet engines. Today, meteorologists providing weather briefings to pilots can advise them on how to avoid ash plumes on their routes.

Because of the opportunities that the eruption presented for the study of volcanoes, the USGS convinced Congress to approve funding for the Cascades Volcano Observatory, headquartered in Vancouver, Washington. A variety of geological specialists—*geochemists* (scientists who study the chemical structure of rocks), *hydrologists* (scientists who study the behavior of fresh water in streams, rivers, and lakes), and *geophysicists* (scientists who study earth movements, tides, and weather)—work together at the observatory to analyze the large amounts of data coming in from sensors and observation stations throughout the Cascade Range. Their goal is to uncover the many secrets of volcanoes.

Data Flows from the 2004 Eruption

The continuous monitoring in place since the 1980 eruption provided the warning for the 2004 eruption. In 2004 scientists were able to respond with many observational and data-collection techniques that had been unavailable in 1980.

Aircraft with special sensors flew near the crater to "sniff" for gases that could indicate that magma was moving near the surface. The National Weather Service used radar to track the larger ash clouds, and thermal imaging equipment detected magma as it moved closer to the surface. Radar from satellites sent information from which any movement of the mountain could be measured. Remote-controlled cameras installed on the crater rim allowed scientists to peer into the volcano without endangering their lives.

The huge increase in data allowed scientists to provide current, accurate information to government agencies and the public while they learned more about volcano behavior. Scientists continue to warn that this new eruptive period could last for weeks or months. Although an explosion equal to the 1980 event is extremely unlikely, Mount St. Helens could erupt explosively with very little warning.

CHAPTER 8

The Legacy of Mount St. Helens

A plume of smoke and ash rises from one of the early May 1980 eruptions of Mount St. Helens. (Photo courtesy of U.S. Geological Survey)

The 1980 Mount St. Helens eruption has left two legacies—one of danger and one of preparation. Just because the volcano is not erupting does not mean it poses no danger. Only two years after the eruption, the danger from potential flooding reached a critical level. The eruption also made people in the Pacific Northwest aware that they needed to be prepared for a future eruption of any of the Cascade Range volcanoes. If they were not prepared, people could die—many more people than those who died as a result of Mount St. Helens.

Remaining Dangers

Spirit Lake's debris dam caused the lake's surface area to double in two years. That might not have been a problem had this naturally occurring dam been stable. But the dam was not stable. Scientists and engineers studying the dam realized that running water was eroding away the ash and smaller bits of rock. If water broke through the dam, 40,000 people living downstream could be in danger. Businesses, factories, a nuclear power plant, the major interstate freeway running through Washington, and the shipping lanes in the Columbia River serving the Port of Portland were also at risk. If another major eruption occurred or if there were a major earthquake near the volcano, the entire dam could collapse, sending a huge wall of water into the valley.

By August 2, 1982, the situation was so critical that Governor John Spellman declared a state of emergency. A Presidential Emergency Declaration for Washington soon followed, issued by President Ronald Reagan on August 19. As a result, FEMA was called in to develop and execute a plan to reduce the flood danger with the cooperation of the USFS, the USGS, and the Army Corps of Engineers.

After careful study, these agencies decided that the best solution would be to create an outlet so the lake water would flow into the south fork of Coldwater Creek. That job would take several years. In the meantime, they had to prevent the lake from getting bigger. The Army Corps of Engineers did so by pumping the water out as fast as it came in. Then the engineers started working on an outlet channel—1.5 miles (2.4 km) of pipe that was 11 feet (3.4 m) in diameter. In October 1982, the engineers started carving out the tunnel for the pipe with a 112-ton (102-mt) tunnel-boring machine. The work was finished in the spring of 1985. The USFS spends over $500,000 per year to maintain the tunnel.

Stabilizing the debris dam removed some of the danger of flooding, but the amount of sediment that had been deposited in the streams and riverbeds reduced the amount of water that could flow within their banks. The rising level of the riverbeds in the Toutle, Cowlitz, and Columbia rivers meant that even a small increase over normal rainfall could cause flooding in low-lying areas. Flooding was not the only problem in the Columbia River. In later years, silt coming down from the mountainside would continue to reduce the water depth and limit the size of ships that sailed upstream to the Port of Portland. The Army Corps of Engineers would need to continue its dredging operations to keep the channel open.

Being Prepared

The coordination problems that plagued local, state, and federal agencies during the first eruptive period have been largely addressed in the past few years. The Cowlitz County Sheriff's Department now coordinates all federal, state, and local agencies that could be called upon to assist residents in danger. The department has created a detailed warning and evacuation system that will move people rapidly out of flood-prone areas. In addition, it has developed a plan to assess the most dangerous areas around the volcano and keep people out.

Since people tend to forget about the possible dangers once an eruptive period has passed, the sheriff's office has also established an extensive program to get information out to residents about warnings, evacuations, and shelters. The office provides advice on how to reduce damage to property, what to do in an emergency, and what steps to take to stay safe during a flood or mudflow. Local newspapers and county offices distribute copies of a flood preparation guide that includes area maps with evacuation routes clearly marked.

These plans will work only if there is advance notice of an eruption. USGS scientists constantly monitor Mount St. Helens for earthquakes, changes in the amount and type of gas emissions, and changes in the volcano's surface (such as large cracks or swelling of the dome). Hydrologists closely monitor the amount of snow and ice on the mountain so they can determine the potential flood danger during an eruption.

Considering that 500,000 people visit the Mount St. Helens area every year, it is also important to get safety information out to visitors. County and state agencies created pamphlets especially for visitors. The pamphlets are available from businesses along the route to the mountain and at the visitor centers within the national forest. Signs lining the road explain the meaning of warning sirens, indicate the radio stations that carry emergency broadcasts, and point out evacuation routes. Although some businesses worried that these safety measures—particularly the signs—would scare tourists away, state officials have made safety a priority. They are convinced that it makes sense to let visitors know that the volcano poses a real danger. USGS scientist Dan Miller noted, "It's only a matter of time before it goes [again]. We'll try to tell people when."

Exploiting Opportunities

The eruption of Mount St. Helens and the concerns that another eruption could occur in any of the volcanoes in the Cascade chain led to the rapid extension of the University of Washington's Seismic Network (the system of seismographs placed throughout the Cascade Range that send signals of ground movement back to the university). Because the network is online and computerized, it can obtain 100 samples of ground movements each second. These data are extremely important for scientists studying earthquakes and volcanism in the Pacific Northwest. The network is also important because it allows scientists to provide emergency agencies with information about potential eruptions that could save lives. (The Mount St. Helens eruption affected response to volcanic eruptions not only in the United States, but also around the world, as described in the "International Effects" sidebar on the following page.)

International Effects

One result of the Mount St. Helens eruption has influenced the response to volcanoes around the world. The USGS and the U.S. Agency for International Development have joined forces to fund the Volcano Disaster Assistance Program. A team from this program was flown to the Philippines when Mount Pinatubo started to show signs of eruption in 1991. The team's hazard map was used to make decisions about evacuations that ultimately prevented the deaths of thousands of people. Since then, teams have assisted with monitoring the Popocatépetl volcano near Mexico City. (This volcano has erupted intermittently since December 1994 and could threaten millions of people.) They have also monitored the Soufrière Hills volcano on the Caribbean Island of Montserrat (which erupted in 1995) and another two dozen volcanoes in Central and South America, the Caribbean, Africa, Asia, and the South Pacific. This program is an example of how scientists involved in research on easing the effects of hazards for nearby populations and those involved with volcano research have worked more closely together since the Mount St. Helens eruption.

In the Cascades, the volcanic eruptions themselves are not much of a danger. Although Mount St. Helens did erupt *out* instead of *up*, that is a rare occurrence. Most eruptions produce a substantial cloud of ash and steam that will be carried away by the wind. The ash then becomes a major problem only if it drifts over a large city. As Spokane and Yakima found out, ash, even in small amounts, very quickly stops engines from running.

The much greater danger is from floods and mudflows. The Cascades are always cloaked in snow and ice, even in the summer. In the winter, they wear a massive amount of snow and ice. If it melts quickly during an eruption, it moves down the mountainside, picking up trees, sediment, and rock debris—also cars, houses, and other human-made objects in the way. Most of the streams that drain these mountains head west, right into the largest cities. The mountain that most emergency officials and scientists consider to be the most dangerous of the Cascade volcanoes is Mount Rainier.

An eruption on Mount Rainier about 5,700 years ago triggered what is known as the Osceola Mudflows. These mudflows quickly moved down the mountainside and finally landed 68 miles (110 km) away. The mud covered approximately 195 square miles (500 km^2). A number of Washington towns are built on this mud, and if a fast-moving lahar were to occur today, it would reach these cities and a number of others in an hour or less. There would be no time to alert residents to evacuate. In fact, in the early 1970s, a USGS report recommended that permanent residences should not be built on some sections of the valley floor near Mount Rainier. The report also recommended that some campgrounds be moved out of low-lying areas and that affected roads and bridges be constructed to survive a direct hit by a major mudflow.

Even if a lahar did not form, melt water from snow could quickly fill up rivers and streams in the area as it rushed toward the Washington cities of Seattle and Tacoma. Rainier would not need to erupt fully to trigger large avalanches and mudflows—a few steam explosions or spots where hot magma has moved toward the surface could have exactly the same effect.

These are not the only areas in danger from the results of a volcanic eruption. Mount Hood—which has done some quaking of its own—is just 45 miles (72 km) east of Portland. In the past, it has erupted at about the same time as Mount St. Helens. In the aftermath of the Mount St. Helens eruption, the town of Sandy, Oregon, which lies within the path of Hood's mudflows, has developed an evacuation plan. Geologists have also found evidence that prehistoric mudflows triggered by Hood's eruptions reached the Portland area—home to over 500,000 people.

As of today, the David A. Johnston Cascades Volcano Observatory (renamed for the geologist killed on Coldwater Ridge) monitors all volcanic activity in the Cascades. The observatory is recognized throughout the world as a leader in volcano research.

CHAPTER 9

Conclusion

After swarms of earthquakes at Mount St. Helens in September 2004, USGS scientist Michael Poland collects information on the eastern side of the mountain. Mount Adams is visible in the distance. (Photo courtesy of Associated Press)

The Mount St. Helens story is both scientifically and politically significant. For scientists in the United States, the eruption provided the opportunity to study a volcano close up without having to fly halfway around the world. Because the eruption virtually stripped bare the immediate surrounding area, it gave biologists a

once-in-a-lifetime chance to observe—in an accelerated way—how life developed on Earth. As Peter Frenzen notes,

> It's a natural experiment, an experiment too expensive and impractical to produce. Imagine the grant request: 'What I want to do is take every bit of vegetation and animal life off 100,000 acres [40,470 ha] of forest and subalpine meadows. And then I want to come in and cover it with a new material so we can monitor returning life.'

No one, of course, would approve such a project, but Mount St. Helens created those conditions in just a few hours.

In addition, because the volcano has continued to be active in a subdued way since the 1980 eruption, USGS geologists have been able to collect massive amounts of data that have changed how earth scientists evaluate the volcanic deposits left by prehistoric eruptions. The same data have also led to changes in the way that volcanic predictions are made. USGS scientist Steven Brantley said, "We've learned to recognize certain patterns that precede eruptions. We can see them coming."

Plants and animals of many species were killed or forced to move out of the Mount St. Helens area by the eruption, but nature's recovery did not start with a mountainside of bare rock. Pockets of life remained scattered throughout the ash, rock, mud, and scorched trees. As these plants and animals struggled to survive, the effect that one species might have on another's ability to thrive became more apparent to researchers. Before the eruption, for example, when plants densely covered the mountain, no one had noticed that the hoof marks in the ground left by elk and deer helped plants to grow. But once the plants were gone, it was obvious that the imprints collected seeds and water, thus encouraging plants to sprout.

Ultimately, volcanoes are a danger only if people live too close to them. When volcanoes that are far from populated or recreational areas erupt, only scientists give them much thought. They are just part of the geological cycle of land formation in which molten rock is brought up from below Earth's surface to create newly hardened rock. Then, over time, the rock erodes, plants and animals move in, and a new ecosystem develops, only to be destroyed and re-created in a later eruption.

In some parts of the world, the fertile soil surrounding volcanoes makes them an irresistible draw to people looking for a good place to grow their crops. In others, like Japan, there are so many volcanoes on such a small patch of land that people do not have the option of moving away from them. In the Pacific Northwest, no one has to live close to the Cascade Range and its volcanoes. Yet these areas are extremely beautiful and boast valuable agricultural land. Visitors must heed the lessons of Mount St. Helens—no volcano is perhaps ever truly extinct, and survival depends on being able to evacuate the area. People need to respect the power of volcanoes and learn to live with them. As clever as people are, they will never be able to control a volcano.

At present, visitors can look directly into the gaping crater of Mount St. Helens and see the rising lava dome 6 miles (9.6 km) away. As loose rocks fall from the sides of the crater, puffs of dust come up. The ash puffs give some visitors the feeling that it may be time to head back down the mountain to safety. But as the fall 2004 eruptions showed, the possibility of seeing a minor eruption up close draws thousands of people to the mountain and its visitor centers. Geologists have been watching the magma move up through the mountain and into the dome—but no one knows when the next explosive eruption will occur.

Over the next several hundred years, the dome will continue to grow, and the rocks from the sides of the crater will continue to fall down as they are loosened by wind, rain, snow, and ice—and the occasional earthquake. The danger of an eruption will always be present. Mount St. Helens will never again be the "Fujiyama of the West," with a perfectly symmetrical cone. But it is likely to always keep another name that it was given by the Klickitat tribe—*Tah-one-lat-clah,* or "Fire Mountain."

Time Line

1980

March 15	Starting this day, within the next week, seismographs will record more than 100 earthquakes in the vicinity of Mount St. Helens
March 20, 3:45 P.M. (PST)	An earthquake with a 4.2 magnitude triggers avalanches on the mountain
March 24	Seismographs record as many as 20 earthquakes per hour
March 25	Seismographs record five earthquakes with magnitudes greater than 4.0 in one hour; a large crack appears in the snow on the summit of Mount St. Helens
March 27, 12:36 P.M. (PST)	Seismographs record more frequent earthquakes; a hole forms in the summit icecap, followed by the sound of an explosion, a puff of ash and steam, a 4.7-magnitude earthquake, and a plume of black ash that reaches 7,000 feet (2,135 m) above the peak; afterward, a crater 200 feet (61 m) in diameter is seen near the peak

Photo courtesy of Associated Press

March 28	Twelve small eruptions occur
March 30	Scientists observe 93 explosions within 24 hours
March 31	Cowlitz County in Washington declares a state of emergency
April 1	Steam and ash plumes rise to 20,000 feet (6,100 m)
April 8	Scientists observe explosive activity for four hours

April 19	Geologists monitoring the mountain's appearance notice a bulge on the north side
May 17	The bulge on the north side of the mountain continues to grow outward; by this time, it is expanding at the rate of 5 feet (1.5 m) per day
May 18, 8:32:20 A.M. (PDT)	A magnitude-5.1 earthquake strikes 1 mile (1.6 km) below the volcano
May 18, 8:32:21 A.M. (PDT)	The bulge on the north flank slides away as the largest recorded landslide in history; it reaches speeds of almost 180 miles (290 km) per hour
May 18, 8:32:45 A.M. (PDT)	An enormous explosion shoots out from the north side of the volcano where the bulge had been; this lateral blast sends rock, ash, and hot gases toward the north; traveling at 730 miles (1,175 km) per hour, the gas, rock, and ash move past the landslide and carry away almost everything in an 8-mile (12.9-km) radius
May 18, 8:34 A.M. (PDT)	Everything within 15 miles (24.1 km) of the blast has been flattened
May 18, 8:35 A.M. (PDT)	Mudflows start down Pine Creek, Muddy River, Swift Creek, the Kalama River, and the South Fork of the Toutle River
May 18, 8:47 A.M. (PDT)	A cloud of ash explodes from the top of the peak and extends 12 miles (19.3 km) into the atmosphere
May 18, 11:45 A.M. (PDT)	The ash cloud reaches Spokane, Washington, 300 miles (480 km) away
May 18, 1:00 P.M. (PDT)	Mudflows carrying 65 million cubic yards (50 million m³) of sediment begin on the North Fork of the Toutle River and continue into the Cowlitz and Columbia rivers

Photo courtesy of Associated Press

Photo courtesy of U.S. Geological Survey

May 18, 3:00 P.M. (PDT)	The Toutle River crests at 21 feet (6.4 m) above normal
May 18, 5:30 P.M. (PDT)	The eruption starts to subside
May 19	The ash cloud arrives in the central United States
May 25, 2:30 A.M. (PDT)	Another eruption sends ash 9 miles (14.5 km) into the atmosphere
June 12, evening	Mount St. Helens sends up two separate ash plumes and erupts lava that begins to form a dome inside the new crater
July 22, 5:14 P.M. (PDT)	A number of eruptions destroy the dome that began building on June 12, and a new one starts to form
August 7, 4:26 P.M. (PDT)	Mount St. Helens emits an 8-mile (12.9-km) high ash plume and pyroclastic flows; the eruption destroys the dome that began building on July 22, and a new one starts to form
October 16–18	An ash cloud extends 10 miles (16 km) into the air, and small pyroclastic flows move down the mountain; the eruption destroys the dome that began building on August 7, and a new one starts to form

Photo courtesy of Associated Press

2001

November 3	Earthquake swarms rock the mountain

2004

September 23–25	Earthquake swarms occur less than 1 mile (1.6 km) beneath the dome
September 26–30	Swarm intensity increases
October 1	A 25-minute eruption sends ash and steam up to 10,000 feet (3,050 m)
October 7–12	Dome building increases
October 13	A new lobe of lava oozes out onto the surface

Chronology of Volcanic Eruptions

The following list is a selection of major volcanic eruptions of the last 150 years.

1856

March 2–17
Awu
Indonesia
About 2,800 killed

1883

August 26
Krakatau
Indonesia
About 36,000 killed

1892

June 7–12
Awu
Indonesia
About 1,500 killed

1902

May 6
La Soufrière
Saint Vincent, British West Indies
About 1,500 killed

May 8
Pelée
Martinique, French West Indies
More than 30,000 killed

October 25
Santa Maria
Guatemala
About 6,000 killed

1906

April 8
Vesuvius
Italy
About 350 killed

1911

January 30
Taal
Philippines
About 1,330 killed

1919

May 19
Kelut
Indonesia
About 5,100 killed

Photo courtesy of Associated Press

1930

November 25

Merapi

Indonesia

About 1,300 killed

1938

May 29

Rabaul

Papua New Guinea

About 500 killed

1951

January 21

Lamington

Papua New Guinea

About 2,900 killed

1953

December 24

Ruapehu

New Zealand

151 killed

1963

May 16

Agung

Indonesia

About 1,100 killed

1966

April 26

Kelut

Indonesia

212 killed

1977

January 10

Nyiragongo

Congo

70 killed

1979

July

Iliwerung

Indonesia

About 500 killed

1980

May 18

Mount St. Helens

United States (Washington)

57 killed

1981

March–April

Semeru

Indonesia

253 killed

Photo courtesy of Associated Press

1982

April 3
El Chichón
Mexico
About 3,500 killed

1985

November 13
Nevado del Ruiz
Colombia
About 23,000 killed

1986

August 26
Nyos
Cameroon
About 1,700 killed

1991

June 15
Pinatubo
Philippines
About 300 killed

1993

February 2–April 4
Mayon
Philippines
75 killed

1997

February 13–May 7
Okmok
Alaska
None killed

1999

**September 30
(still active 2004)**
Tungurahua
Ecuador
None killed (22,000 evacuated)

2002

May 13 (still active 2004)
Anatahan
Mariana Islands
None killed (permanent residents evacuated in June 2003)

2003

March 18
Barren Island
Andaman Islands, India
None killed

2004

June 8
Bromo
Indonesia
2 killed
June 10
Awu
Indonesia
None killed (12,000 evacuated)

Photo courtesy of Associated Press

Glossary

active   Describes a volcano that has any kind of geological activity associated with it

amphibians   Animals, such as frogs and salamanders, that can live both in and out of the water

ash   The smallest particles—less than 0.2 inches (4 mm) in diameter—ejected by volcanoes

ash fall   The result of ash being blown into the atmosphere and then "raining" down on land below

crater   A bowl-shaped area at the top of a volcano

debris flow   Earth material that moves rapidly downhill as a result of becoming saturated with water; often, it is triggered by large amounts of rain; during volcanic eruptions, it can be triggered by rapidly melting snow and ice

dome   A rounded mound of lava that looks like the top of a mushroom, formed when lava is too thick and sticky to flow

dormant   Describes a volcano that is not currently active but could become active because of its geologic features

erosion   The wearing away of Earth's surface

extinct   Describes a volcano that has not erupted in tens of thousands of years and is no longer near an area of seismic activity

flood   The spreading of water outside of the banks of a river or stream

hatchery   A place where fish are raised from eggs and then released back into the wild to increase fish populations

hot spot   A location on Earth's surface where magma pushes up through a weak section of the crust, forming a volcano

hummock   A large mound of dirt and rock on Earth's surface

lahar   An Indonesian term used to include both debris flows and mudflows

lateral blast   An eruption that explodes out of a volcano's side

lava   Magma that has reached Earth's surface during a volcanic eruption

magma   Molten rock beneath Earth's surface, containing large amounts of gas

mudflow   A mixture of earth and water that moves rapidly down a hillside

mycorrhizal fungus   Fungus found in the ground that provides plants with the nitrogen that they need to grow

pumice   A light-colored, lightweight rock formed when foamy lava cools quickly

pyroclastic   From the Greek "fire broken," refers to material that is ejected from an erupting volcano

pyroclastic flows   Avalanches of extremely hot gas, ash, rock, and glass fragments that are blown out of a volcanic vent and move rapidly down the side of the volcano while hugging the ground; also known as hot avalanches, ignimbrites, or *nuées ardentes* ("glowing clouds" in French)

Richter scale   A numerical scale used to describe the amount of shaking during an earthquake; the larger the number, the more the earth has moved

rift zone   The area where two tectonic plates are pulling apart; this leaves an opening in the crust and allows volcanoes to develop

seismograph   A scientific instrument that measures the strength of earthquakes

subterranean   Beneath Earth's surface

succession   The process whereby areas cleared of plants are slowly recolonized over time, first by small plants (such as grasses) and then by larger plants, until trees come to fill the landscape

swarms   Earthquakes that occur in one area at the rate of hundreds in a day

tephra   Pyroclastic material that moves through the air; tephra is classified depending on its size and composition; ash is the smallest form of tephra

vent   An opening in Earth's surface that erupts rocks and lava

Further Reading and Web Sites

Alaska Volcano Observatory (AVO). This web site has current details on volcanoes in Alaska and on Russia's Kamchatka Peninsula. Available online. URL: http://www.avo.alaska.edu. Accessed April 26, 2004.

American Red Cross—Disaster Services. This web site provides information on the dangers of volcanoes and other disasters and how to remain safe. Available online. URL: http://www.redcross.org/services/disaster/0,1082,0_501_,00.html. Accessed April 26, 2004.

Anderson, Ross. "Mount St. Helens remembered: 'God is speaking.'" *Seattle Times,* May 14, 2000. Residents of the town of Ritzville in eastern Washington recall what happened to them after the eruption of Mount St. Helens. Available online. URL: http://seattletimes.nwsource.com/helens/story1.html. Accessed June 24, 2004.

Annenberg/CPB Learner.org—Volcanoes: Can We Predict Volcanic Eruptions? This web site contains information on types of volcanoes, the hazards that they present, and the risks to people. Includes video clips of volcanoes. Available online. URL: http://www.learner.org/exhibits/volcanoes/entry.html. Accessed April 26, 2004.

Bardintzeff, Jacques-Marie and Alexander R. McBirney. *Volcanology.* Boston: Jones & Bartlett Publishers, 2000. This book discusses volcanic processes and the impact of volcanoes on people and the environment.

Carson, Rob. *Mount St. Helens: The Eruption and Recovery of a Volcano.* Seattle: Sasquatch Books, 1990. This book discusses the events leading up to the 1980 eruption, the eruption itself, and nature's recovery in the months that followed.

Dartmouth College—The Electronic Volcano. Includes information on volcanoes around the world, photographs, diagrams,
and maps. Introductory material can be accessed in several
languages. Available online. URL: http://www.dartmouth
.edu/~volcano/. Accessed April 26, 2004.

Duffield, Wendell A. *Chasing Lava: A Geologist's Adventures
at the Hawaiian Volcano Observatory.* Missoula, Mont.:
Mountain Press Publishing Company, 2003. This book
describes the author's three years studying the Hawaiian
volcano Kilauea.

Federal Emergency Management Agency (FEMA)—Backgrounder:
Volcanoes. This web site provides information on the dangers
posed by volcanoes, how to prepare for an eruption, and what
to do after one occurs. Available online. URL: http://www
.fema.gov/hazards/volcanoes/volcano.shtm. Accessed April 26,
2004.

Findley, Rowe. "Mount St. Helens." *National Geographic,*
May 2000, 106. This article describes the natural recovery
in the vicinity of Mount St. Helens in the 20 years after its
eruption.

Mohlenbrock, Robert H. "Mount St. Helens, Washington."
Natural History, July/August 1990, 26. Ten years after the
Mount St. Helens eruption, Mohlenbrock describes the
changes that occurred in the landscape and in animal
and plant life immediately after the eruption. He also
tells how nature is healing the scars left behind by
the volcano.

National Park Service (NPS)—Hawai'i Volcanoes National
Park. This web site provides extensive information on the
Hawai'i Volcanoes National Park on the Big Island of
Hawaii, home of the world's most active volcano—Kilauea.
Available online. URL: http://www.nps.gov/havo/. Accessed
April 26, 2004.

Ota, Alan K., John Snell, and Leslie L. Zaitz. "A Terrible Beauty: Mount St. Helens Special Report." *The Oregonian,* V1–V40. October 27, 1980. Assembled by staff reporters who covered the story of Mount St. Helens from the first rumblings, this report includes excellent photographs and interviews with government officials, rescuers, and survivors.

Rosenfeld, Charles, and Robert Cooke. *Earthfire: The Eruption of Mount St. Helens.* Cambridge, Mass.: Massachusetts Institute of Technology Press, 1982. This book gives detailed information on the eruption of Mount St. Helens, including the effect of ash falls on nature and people.

Rosi, Mauro, Paulo Papale, Luca Lupi, and Marco Stoppato. English translation by Jay Hyam. *Volcanoes (Firefly Guide).* Toronto: Firefly Books, 2003. This book provides details on 100 active volcanoes around the world.

San Diego State University Department of Geological Sciences— How Volcanoes Work. This web site provides a lot of scientific information for students and teachers about volcanic features and processes. Available online. URL: http://www .geology.sdsu.edu/how_volcanoes_work/. Accessed April 24, 2004.

Sigurdsson, Haraldur, Bruce Houghton, Hazel Rymer, John Stix, and Steve McNutt. *Encyclopedia of Volcanoes.* San Diego: Academic Press, 1999. This book is a comprehensive work on volcanoes with contributions from over 100 volcano experts from around the world.

Thompson, Dick. *Volcano Cowboys: The Rocky Evolution of a Dangerous Science.* New York: St. Martin's Press, 2002. The book describes the lives of volcanologists as they go about their work trying to figure out why volcanoes behave the way they do.

Turner, Monica G. "Fires, Hurricanes and Volcanoes: Comparing Large Disturbances." *Bioscience,* November 1997, 758. This article examines how three different natural disasters—fires, hurricanes, and volcanoes—affect the environment. Also covers the differences in recovery rates from these disasters.

University of North Dakota—Volcano World. This web site allows users to get information about volcanoes sorted by location, description, and name. Users may also send questions to a volcanologist. Available online. URL: http://volcano.und.nodak.edu/vw.html. Accessed April 26, 2004.

U.S. Forest Service (USFS)—Mount St. Helens National Volcanic Monument. This web site provides detailed information on the monument, including the history of the volcano and nature's recovery after the eruption. Includes many photographs and a webcam image of the mountain that updates every five minutes. Available online. URL: http://www.fs .fed.us/gpnf/mshnvm/. Accessed April 26, 2004.

U.S. Geological Survey (USGS)—Cascades Volcano Observatory. This web site includes links to current information about volcanoes all over the world. Available online. URL: http:// vulcan.wr.usgs.gov. Accessed April 26, 2004.

U.S. Geological Survey (USGS) Volcano Hazards Program. This web site provides up-to-date information on U.S. and Russian volcanoes, as well as weekly updates on volcanoes around the world. Includes emergency planning advice and discusses warning systems. Available online. URL: http:// volcanoes.usgs.gov/. Accessed April 26, 2004.

Zebrowski, Ernest. *The Last Days of St. Pierre: The Volcanic Disaster That Claimed 30,000 Lives.* New Brunswick, N.J.: Rutgers University Press, 2002. This book is a well-documented account of the events occurring before, during, and after the 1902 eruption of Mont Pelée that wiped out the city of St. Pierre on the Caribbean island of Martinique.

Index